# ARCHITECTURAL DIGEST    AMERICAN INTERIORS

# AMERICAN INTERIORS

ARCHITECTURAL DIGEST PRESENTS A DECADE

OF IMAGINATIVE RESIDENTIAL DESIGN

EDITED BY PAIGE RENSE

EDITOR-IN-CHIEF, ARCHITECTURAL DIGEST

THE KNAPP PRESS    PUBLISHERS    LOS ANGELES

Published in the United States of America in 1978
The Knapp Press
5900 Wilshire Boulevard, Los Angeles, California 90036
Copyright © 1978 by Knapp Communications Corporation
All rights reserved
First Edition

Library of Congress Cataloging in Publication Data:
Main entry under title: Architectural digest American interiors
1. Interior decoration—United States. I. Rense, Paige.
II. Architectural digest. III. Title: American interiors.
NK2004.A7      747′.8′80973      77-23652

ISBN 0−89535−022−5
Printed and bound in the United States of America

# CONTENTS

# FOREWORD

How do you choose from among the best? That difficult question faced us as we compiled AMERICAN INTERIORS, a collection of thirty-five outstanding interior designs that have appeared in *Architectural Digest*.

As editor-in-chief, I view over one thousand houses a year, of which a small number find their way to the pages of *Architectural Digest*. People often ask me what I look for in a home. My answer is: I look for magic.

This is a compendium of that magic. It seemed to us that these designs merited unified presentation in book form. Their unity does not come from similarity; the houses cover a wide range of styles, tastes and locations, sometimes with these factors in unorthodox combinations. From a design point of view, this collection tells of diversity — of a multiplicity of choices, obstacles overcome and possibilities maximized. From a human point of view, it tells of people who know how they want to live and who are willing to risk inventing their own environment. The magic happens when these two points of view coincide.

Once the right interiors are found, there is another challenge to be met: The design must "read" photographically. Homes, like people, are sometimes just not photogenic. There are instances when the impact of an interior eludes the camera's eye. Just as we have sought the world's leading interior designers, we have sought the world's most gifted photographers. The presentation, too, must have magic.

As *Architectural Digest* has grown, we have sometimes mistakenly been called "arbiters of taste." We are not arbiters, but reporters, conveying what leading designers create, and how people of taste and style live. The subject matter of each feature article in *Architectural Digest* is usually limited to a single place and time.

But we are reporters with a difference. Our news does not stop being new. I have been astonished, reviewing homes that have appeared in our pages over the past few years, at how these interior designs defy a date. In what other field could a journalistic compendium spanning a decade not become a series of mere period pieces? Last year's fashions no longer command attention. Last month's politics is trivia. Yesterday's humor ceases to amuse. Even in interior design, fads and trends quickly appear awkward and contrived.

It is the element of magic that keeps these thirty-five interiors continually surprising and fresh. They seem to remain new and gain impact with each viewing. The subtleties of their design only clarify with time, as line and form and balances unfold. Antiques and works of art become ever more beautiful and precious. A home built with humanity and sensitivity will be of compelling interest always. *continued*

I hope that people will read AMERICAN INTERIORS for many different reasons, for there is much here to absorb. Among other things, I believe this collection gives a clear picture of our taste in the United States. I believe, however, that this picture will not become just a quaint time capsule, but that the magic of these American interiors will continue to stimulate, delight and inspire.

Paige Rense
Editor-in-Chief
Los Angeles, California

# ARCHITECTURAL DIGEST  AMERICAN INTERIORS

# CONSUELO VANDERBILT BALSAN'S PALM BEACH RESIDENCE

The life of Consuelo Vanderbilt Balsan, who died at the age of eighty-seven, was a life of sorrow and of joy, of glitter and gold, of wealth and obligation. It was, perhaps more than any of these, a life of compelling symbolism, spanning as it did eras so far removed from each other in time and in spirit. She grew up in the world of Queen Victoria and died in the contemporary United States.

Like her one-time relation Sir Winston Churchill, who rode at the battle of Omdurman with Lord Kitchener and then lived on to witness man's exploration and conquest of space, Mme Balsan's life was characterized by the extremes of history. The daughter of William K. Vanderbilt, she was married in 1895, at the age of eighteen and very much in opposition to her wishes, to the duke of Marlborough. "I spent the morning of my wedding day," she wrote in her memoirs, "in tears and alone."

Nevertheless, endowed with a sense of courage and natural graciousness, she managed to play her role as duchess of Marlborough with grace and charm, visiting Queen Victoria at Windsor Castle and entertaining the future King Edward VII at Blenheim Palace, the seat of the Marlboroughs. In those years her aristocratic beauty was captured by artists like John Singer Sargent and Paul-César Helleu, and it was a beauty that lasted, only gently brushed by time, until her death.

In 1921 she was finally able to marry for love, and thereafter she and her husband, Colonel Jacques Balsan, lived for the most part in France, dividing their time between a rustic château in Normandy and a house at Eze in the south of France. When Paris fell to the Germans in 1940, she and her husband came to the United States to live.

They were accustomed to spend half the year in one of two large houses: *Old Fields* on Long Island, and *Casa Alva* in Florida, which Mme Balsan began building in the 1930s. After the death of her husband she followed a similar pattern, except that she moved to smaller houses, one of which was in Southampton and the other in Palm Beach.

Built in the 1940s, her new home in Palm Beach was designed in the manner of a townhouse and is separated from the street by a high hedge. The first floor contains staff rooms, service areas and garages. Mme Balsan's living and entertainment areas were on the second floor, and bedrooms occupied the third floor. The scale of the rooms is generous, with high ceilings and fine architectural detailing.

Though the house was considerably smaller than those to which she had been accustomed, her way of life remained essentially the same. She still surrounded herself with the furniture and paintings and antiques she had collected for so many years. Many of them, in fact, had come with her from Europe in 1940, and it had always been her custom to carry favorite objects back and forth from house to house, from country to country. She now carried her collections from New York to Florida. And so it continued until the end of her life.

When Mme Balsan moved from Southampton for her annual stay of six months in Palm Beach, she saw that each of her favorite pieces was shipped with a careful label on it, indicating the exact position it was to occupy: the paintings by Fragonard, Cézanne, Renoir, Utrillo; the Aubusson and Savonnerie rugs; the bronzes; the Régence and Louis XV furniture; the fine collections of Meissen and Ch'ien Lung porcelain.

She had grown up with, and acquired through the years, these fine antiques and period pieces, and naturally they found places in her last home in Palm Beach. Yet nothing she chose to live with suggested a museum or served only to recall some vanished moment of the past. Consuelo Vanderbilt Balsan was far too vital, and far too American, for that. Yet she possessed a refined sense of civilization and of tradition. The stage was still elaborate, though now, in Palm Beach, it was on a smaller scale. As always, her personality shone through the house, and that personality was not elaborate. There was in her not only an appreciation of beauty and quality, but a realist's love of practicality.

"Louis XV furniture is extremely comfortable," she used to say, and the remark can hardly be interpreted as an apology.

The beauty of her Palm Beach home, it must be said, did not come simply—or perhaps in any way—from the rare antiques and the fine paintings and the china collections. It came, rather, from herself: from her particular artistry of conception and arrangement; from her concern as a hostess and friend; from love. She saw that each room glowed, not alone with antiques and charming bibelots, but with the more perishable beauty of the flowers she delighted in placing in such generous quantities throughout every room of the house.

Her taste was not acquired, not learned. It had been there from the beginning. In the dining room of the Palm Beach house, for example, it was her habit to place a profusion of pink chrysanthemums to grace the black-lacquered cabinet and the small chairs that had once been in the Tuileries. Inside her house, the atmosphere was quite as bright as it was outdoors where the Florida sun warmed other flowers and a multitude of subtropical trees.

Consuelo Vanderbilt Balsan had lived in many houses in many different countries—from Blenheim Palace to a French château to a final and relatively small home in Palm Beach—but the imprint of her personality had been on all of them. It was not the imprint of grandeur nor wealth nor aristocracy. In spite of her long years in Europe, to the end she was an American, and her taste, if not precisely simple, was entirely unaffected. She had preferred love to being the duchess of Marlborough, and there was no doubt that she preferred people and friends and flowers to inanimate objects, however rare or costly. It was simply that she had them all.

No amount of wealth and no multitude of possessions, however, can guarantee beauty or personality or ultimate refinement. These are qualities of the spirit, which Mme Balsan carried with her throughout a long, glamorous and extremely multi-faceted life that led from the court of Queen Victoria to present-day America.

The very rich may be different from you and me, as F. Scott Fitzgerald suggested in his writings, but they necessarily share the human condition. Like some of us, they can be cruel and ostentatious; insecure and unsuccessful. Like others of us, they may have a genuine love of life and a natural refinement of spirit. Consuelo Vanderbilt Balsan was always in the latter category.

An atmosphere of splendor
distinguishes the elegant Palm
Beach townhouse of the late
Consuelo Vanderbilt Balsan.
Originally intended for formal
parties and receptions, the
elaborate Drawing Room's
gracious proportions are
extended by mirrored walls at
each end of the room that are
punctuated with Ionic columns.
Fine Louis XVI pieces—a
giltwood canapé and four
fauteuils signed by Jacob—form
a seating arrangement, while
a Chinese tortoiseshell-inlaid
lacquer cabinet and a Louis XV
chinoiserie silk screen further
ornament the setting. A grisaille
by Tiepolo on the mirrored
wall and a painting from the
school of Lancret enhance the
18th-century flavor. Silk
draperies, defining a doorway to
another room, resemble a
window treatment.

LEFT: *Another view of the Drawing Room reveals the symmetry of the architectural detailing and the carefully balanced floor plan. By virtue of its size, color and motif, the fine Savonnerie rug unifies the disparate elements within the 50-foot-long room; its circular medallion and the crystal chandelier suspended directly above establish the strong central axis of the design.*

ABOVE: *Though less formal than the drawing room, the Dining Room is no less luxuriously appointed. Emphasis is placed on the center of the room where an axis is again created by the medallion of another Savonnerie rug, as well as a circular Louis XVI mahogany table and a Louis XV crystal chandelier. A Louis XV marble mantel surrounds an intricate metal fireplace and supports a gilt-framed mirror of the same period; the biscuit de Sèvres clock and a pair of candlesticks on the mantel are Louis XVI. A note of lightness is interjected by the presence of a set of cane-backed Régence chairs.*

*An early Savonnerie rug brings vitality to the Sitting Room. Two pairs of Louis XV bergères support Mme Balsan's contention that the furniture of this period is comfortable as well as elegant. Other Louis XV and Louis XVI furnishings embellish the room; particularly fine is a marquetry bureau à cylindre inlaid with mother-of-pearl and signed A.L. Gilbert.*

In the Bedroom, flower-strewn French chintz,
French Impressionist paintings and Oriental objets
d'art create an environment of lightness and
delicacy, while a golden glow radiates from the
Imperial Chinese rug with Taoist symbols.
Highlights of the room include a Georgian
chinoiserie drop-front secretary and the silk
brocade-upholstered Louis XV armchair beside it.

# CONTEMPORARY CONDOMINIUM IN PALM SPRINGS

Rarely does an interior designer have the complete freedom to create a house or apartment from the very beginning: to oversee every detail from outdoor landscaping and electrical systems to sheets on the bed and soap in the guest bathroom.

When Sigmund E. Edelstone decided to buy a small California condominium—in reality, two joined together—at The Racquet Club located in Palm Springs, it seemed almost inevitable for him to seek the assistance of Harold Broderick, president of Arthur Elrod Associates.

The design firm, engaged in projects all over the country, has its main offices in Palm Springs. More important, Mr. Edelstone's Chicago apartment had been decorated by the same firm, and he was comfortable with Harold Broderick's approach.

On the surface the Palm Springs condominium seemed a simple enough project. Even with a double unit, the space was modest—some 1,800 square feet—and it was to be used only during the winter months. Mr. Broderick's work, however, took almost a year to complete, and the project was never simple. The constant care and attention required can be attributed to the enthusiasm and the meticulous natures of both owner and interior designer.

Concern with the smallest detail, and an unflagging search for quality, mark the finished product. Mr. Edelstone knew precisely what he wanted: a contemporary home appropriate to the desert, with the California flair typical of a Harold Broderick design. He wanted, as well, a suitable background for an extensive collection of contemporary art in the process of being commissioned, and a comfortable setting in which to entertain with flexibility. Dinner parties often range from four guests to thirty, and the condominium had to accommodate these variations with ease.

The result, quite literally, is the work of many fine artists and master craftsmen, with features not often found in even the most expensive and elaborate homes. All doors, for example, were made by a cabinetmaker, and electrical systems and controls were also custom-made. "They are unique," as the designer says, and every detail is one of a kind. Outdoor sculpture and paintings for the interior were privately commissioned. A soaring metal sculpture by Alexander Liberman is poolside. Several striking primitive objets d'art were chosen to complement the contemporary works. The complex lighting was specially installed, and Harold Broderick himself designed most of the furniture—indeed, nearly everything else, even the plumbing fixtures.

Personalized and individually designed, the Palm Springs condominium has few peers. No ordinary stencil was cut, and there is little in Mr. Edelstone's winter home that can be found elsewhere. This makes for a certain intriguing cachet, as well as for a satisfying unity of design.

In many ways it is an illustration of an essential, and one of Mr. Broderick's favorite requirements of interior design: "The ability to direct your creative concept to the needs and desires of a truly individual client." Such an ability, he feels, is the hallmark of the professional.

Seated behind an uncluttered desk in his Los Angeles office, Mr. Broderick remembers the Edelstone project with a good deal of affection. He is a careful man, not given to excess or dramatic statement, but he takes obvious pride and pleasure in the challenge of "total design" that the project offered. It was a rare opportunity.

From the beginning he was given, at the owner's insistence, nothing more nor less than the opportunity of working with pure space. And surely this must be every interior designer's secret dream. The Racquet Club condominiums were in the process of being built, and it was easy enough to stop construction of Mr. Edelstone's two units when they were no more than shells.

The designer's work began at this point. For the outside he provided landscaping and a pool. And naturally he was responsible for the interior. It was his task to obtain the finest craftsmen available for woodwork, for bathroom marble and for electrical installations. The totality of his involvement extended from large and important pieces of furniture to sheets and towels and tablecloths.

In the dining room, for example, there is a handsome buffet of considerable style and ingenuity, which he designed himself. It is a protean creation. There is complete storage space for flatware and other silver pieces in a cabinet lined with tarnish-preventing cloth, along with a stainless-steel top for serving, recessed outlets for hot trays, clever underlighting and two concealed stereo speakers. The dining room walls are accented by the contemporary paintings of artists Dan Christensen and Charles Hinman.

The bedroom, too, is an illustration of efficient and thoughtful design. A bedside panel contains a master control panel that operates all the lighting as well as music and television. An ingenious desk unit neatly conceals the television, record storage, business machines, file drawers and even a waste basket. Every convenience has been provided for and integrated into the condominium's overall design.

In spite of what might seem an excessive attention to detail, the finished house is surprisingly casual, and quite in keeping with the informal resort setting. Tones of camel and beige suggest the desert, and bright accents of red and brown emphasize the California feeling. It is an eminently usable house—one in which to be comfortable, to entertain effortlessly, and to have the necessary leisure for the enjoyment of contemporary art and the breathtaking natural beauty of the surroundings.

In fact, the house is something of a paradox, at once contemporary and classic, informal and precise. And perhaps symbolic of the paradox are those extraordinary gates and doors of stainless steel, welcoming the visitor to the comfortable world inside. Contemporary as they may be, they nevertheless reflect the bright eternal desert sky and the sand and the high mountains. So this condominium is an intriguing blend of old and new, a mixture of nature and technology. There is no doubt that Harold Broderick has created a design that cannot easily be duplicated, but from which a good deal may be learned. The result seems simple, not in the least contrived. It is beneath the surface, however— in the attention to detail and the endless time spent in preparation—that the design appears in its true complexity. The lightest and cleanest strokes must be made with the surest hand, and the apparent simplicity of the design leaves little room for error.

OPPOSITE: *The gleaming stainless-steel gates and front door of Mr. Sigmund Edelstone's Palm Springs winter haven reflect the extraordinary light and sky of the desert. Interior designer Harold Broderick tempered their modernness by using a classical material, travertine, for the floor of the Entrance Court.* RIGHT: *A bold, painted steel sculpture by Alexander Liberman basks poolside; its pronounced vertical thrust directs attention to the nearby San Jacinto Mountains and visually links the highly textured, blue-toned mountains to the reflective surface of the water. Irregular in shape, the pool is punctuated by a multiplicity of angles and corners.* BELOW RIGHT: *A warm, subtly modulated color study by contemporary artist Robert Natkin is the focal point of the Entrance Hall adjoining the living room. The desert has been brought indoors—walls, ceilings and floor take tones from the environment.*

Sunlight floods through vertical blinds into the Living Room, casting shadows that alter continuously during the course of a day. Sunlight, shadows and the mountain view are important elements in the design. The travertine floor and subtly textured upholstered pieces comprise a deliberately simplified and unobtrusive environment for the natural drama and for a growing collection of contemporary art.

Works of art lend contemporary drama to the Dining Room; the minimal décor is crisp and clean. A large Dan Christensen painting dominates one wall and a shaped canvas by Charles Hinman is the highlight of another. Beneath the Hinman and related to it in scale is a meticulously custom-designed buffet, cantilevered and underlit, whose sleek lines conceal its multiple assets: stereo speakers, stainless-steel surface to facilitate serving, recessed outlets for hot trays, and flatware storage space.

OPPOSITE: *For the versatile Study, Mr. Broderick conceived a stereo and television cabinet that also functions as a dramatic showcase for sculpture; an African carved gazelle head fills the niche. A painting by Voy Fangor provides a colorful note and echoes the use of red in the adjacent master bedroom. Furniture is again neutral in color and simple in line, softened by rounded corners and accented by smooth stainless steel and plexiglass.*

ABOVE RIGHT AND RIGHT: *The Master Bedroom is an oasis of color in the Edelstone condominium, with bold paintings by John Seery and Ilya Bolotowsky, and bright red fabric covering bed and desk chair. It is also a room that benefits greatly from modern technology and careful planning. The recessed bedside panel controls lights, television, stereo, the position of the bed itself. Equally ingenious is a desk unit devised to conceal a television set and record storage, business machines and file drawers.*

# LANDMARK
# FARMHOUSE
# IN
# MANHATTAN

It comes as something of a shock to find a wooden farmhouse on Manhattan's Upper East Side, complete with slightly sagging porch and overgrown front yard. Built in 1835, on what was then the Carnegie estate, this weathered clapboard structure would appear to be more at home fronting the sea in some suitable southern town like Biloxi, Mississippi, or smothered under tumbles of bougainvillaea in sun-drenched Key West.

This oddity, now a New York City historical landmark, has been owned for a number of years by interior designer Thomas A. Morrow III. He has cared for it and restored it with love and devotion.

"When I first moved in," he says, "the house was a complete mess, to say the least. The previous owners had died some years earlier, and everything was literally falling to pieces."

But Mr. Morrow is nothing if not enterprising, and in the evident neglect and decay he saw many positive possibilities for improvement.

"Usually in old houses there are hundreds of coats of paint," he explains, "and the wallpaper is inches thick. But here there was only the original paint and the eighteenth-century wallpaper to change. Fortunately, the moldings were in perfect condition, and so too were the original floors. They had been untouched for years, but they were still a lovely rich wood parquet."

After obtaining some friendly advice from interior designer Albert Hadley, who worked out basic architectural changes, Mr. Morrow set to work on designing the interior. It was never his purpose to remodel the house in any extensive way. Rather, he wished to revitalize its past in the best way possible, to maintain the integrity of the house. To this end he used fabrics and wallcoverings from his own design firm of Hannett-Morrow.

"I don't think you can call this a typical interior designer's home," he says. "I wanted something simple and tranquil, not a display case for my own work. You see, I am surrounded with color all day long, and the effect I was looking for in this house was one of quiet and harmony. The solution was simple enough, and I used earth tones and natural shades. I find the effect very relaxing for me."

In the course of his renovations he studied the original structure with care and came to a number of conclusions. He eliminated certain of the doors and simplified the architectural detailing of many of the rooms, for the most part covering walls in chocolate vinyl with a moiré pattern.

"The furniture itself isn't really too important," the designer says. "I was simply satisfied to pick up neutral colors in the upholstery fabrics, in my own way trying to preserve and heighten the early-Victorian flavor and mood of the house."

In spite of dismissing the redesigning with a seemingly casual approach, Mr. Morrow did find that some important structural changes were required. For example, several long hallways connected the house to an adjoining residence. These odd additions dated from the 1920s and involved a considerable amount of redesigning.

"Actually the whole thing was a sort of long storage tunnel," explains Mr. Morrow. "So several fairly extensive changes were necessary. I had to build a staircase leading to my bedroom upstairs in order to leave the original staircase available as a private entrance for my tenants on the top floors."

In the original entrance hall there was—the reasons for it quite lost in history—a large laundry tub, which the designer enclosed and transformed into a miniature bar. The entire area is now painted in a jungle design, complete with parrots. The painting is his own work, for the fact is that Mr. Morrow is not only a designer but an accomplished artist as well. His work has been shown in New York and Los Angeles, and he has established a reputation as a designer of posters. Indeed, not far from the entrance hall is the studio, filled with posters, drawing tables and piles of fabric, where he and his partner A.T. Hannett work.

It is in the downstairs part of the house that the most extensive restorations took place. The remodeling was time-consuming, and the kitchen and the dining room—in the designer's enigmatic words—"took a lot of work." Ceilings had to be heightened, and the whole area was virtually rebuilt. The dining room now has great rustic charm and is certainly in harmony with the past history of the house. There are pine cupboards, Canadian pine floors, round chairs cushioned in a cheerful print and a large metal cow painted gold that once was a barn weathervane. There is a huge fireplace, and the original rough stone walls are still intact.

"We had the fireplace sandblasted," says the designer. "And then we realized that we had to somehow age the brick again. Otherwise, it would have looked like paper printed with a brick design!"

Beyond the kitchen there is a small garden, in a way rather formal, with a grapevine-covered arbor and masses of roses, tiger lilies and patterned flagstones. It becomes more and more difficult to remember that Mr. Morrow's house lies in the middle of a busy and frantic metropolis. But he has made every effort to maintain the rural charm of the past, although some effects are indeed impossible.

"For example," he says, "it's rather insane to try to have a traditional lawn in the city. The idea did occur to me, but I had to reject it. Anyway, I think the flagstones look more interesting. And they're certainly much easier to keep in shape. The front garden, with its rows of daffodils, daisies and crocuses is an unexpected vision in New York and the indoor winter garden or conservatory was designed as an extra special treat."

The charm of the garden serves to enhance the bedrooms overlooking it, and in them the designer has used colorful fabrics to further the country feeling. For example, the antique bed in the guest room is covered in an airy quilted print repeated—unquilted and unglazed—in wall and window coverings. A blue-and-white print enlivens the master bedroom—it covers the bed and then is reversed for a change of pace in the cupboards—as the charm of the past is restored and enriched.

"It's the kind of house in which to relax and be comfortable," says the designer. "Because now it's one of New York's historic landmarks, I can't change the front. And certainly I wouldn't want to, since I think the whole appeal would be lost. I did put an air conditioner in the front window, however, but there haven't been any complaints. So there are still small things to finish. You know that a house like this is never really completed."

RIGHT: *The greenery of the garden and the front porch of designer Thomas A. Morrow III's wooden farmhouse are an unlikely vision for uptown Manhattan.* BELOW: *The lily painting by Arthur T. Hannett II and a large Tobias Strenover bird painting provide an interesting counterpoint to the controlled brown-and-white scheme of two adjacent 15-by-20-foot Living Rooms.*

Adjoining Living Rooms, typical of the era, feature Victorian marble mantels installed in 1899. BELOW: *Two German carved-wood deer and a pair of Italian candlesticks share one mantel with a basket of bright flowers.* BELOW RIGHT: *A trio of Chinese Export urns adorns the other mantel. Porcelain garden stools topped with mollusk shells heighten the balanced composition.*

LEFT: *Another of Tobias Strenover's paintings of fowl hangs on the moiré-patterned Living Room wallcovering. The small bird-feather painting is from Neuschwanstein Castle, and an early-Victorian horse that had been a child's toy stands proudly on the 1920s table. Subtly related geometric-patterned fabrics cover the contemporary sofa and pair of large pillows.*

In the Library, a group of papier-mâché chairs, circa 1830, surround an impressive glass-topped Regency mahogany rent table decorated with mirror insets and inlaid brass. Three walls are lined with bookshelves, while a group of drawings created by the designer and his friends are arranged on the fourth wall. On the mantel are two vividly colored Bristol prism candlesticks.

ABOVE LEFT: *A French café mirror and paintings by friends complement the faux-bamboo chest in the Master Bedroom.* BELOW LEFT: *In the Guest Room, Victorian tinsel paintings and a large canvas by Tobias Strenover harmonize with the floral-patterned fabric covering the walls and the Directoire bed.* ABOVE: *The garden at the back of the house is filled with a profusion of flowering plants and an arbor entwined with grapevines.*

The rustic ambience of the Dining Room was enhanced after the restoration of original stone walls and Canadian pine floors, the heightening of ceilings and the addition of beams. Hanging baskets, a pine cupboard and cheerful red-white-and-blue print fabrics increase the country mode. Above the hearth is a metal cow that was once a barn weathervane at Sarah Lawrence College.

The Conservatory, with its airy atmosphere and leafy accents, was conceived as a pleasant retreat from the pressures of the city. The 10-foot slope of its roof is dramatized by hanging plants. Terracotta tile floors, wicker furniture with lattice-patterned cushions and ceramic garden stools combine to create a small "Winter Garden" that perpetuates the feeling of the Victorian era.

# A DRAMATIC
# SMALL SPACE
# ODYSSEY

Not long ago, a group of curious and interested people gathered in a small apartment at the top of Nob Hill in San Francisco. The event was a cocktail party unveiling the work of a new interior designer, and the guests had in common uncompromising standards of taste and a low tolerance for imperfection or for the ordinary.

Billy Gaylord, the young interior designer, was understandably nervous before the party. Nevertheless, having worked independently for two years, he felt the time had come to make an initial gesture and begin that slippery ascent in the competitive hierarchy of the design world. In order to make the gesture, he had chosen to show his own recently completed apartment—small, inexpensively furnished, and designed in a matter of weeks. The stakes were high, and it did occur to him that he had been rash and premature. The reactions of the tastemakers he had invited, people who had seen almost everything and whose sophisticated ennui was difficult to jar, could launch his career in splendor—or destroy it completely.

"I did what every young decorator does at first," says Mr. Gaylord. "Perhaps unconsciously, I think we all start with what might be called a 'white period,' when we don't use colors and when we don't take—maybe are afraid to take—a positive position. Somehow it seems safer that way. But, oddly enough, things turned out quite differently in my case. My apartment is positive, perhaps too positive. Not that it was planned that way. As a matter of fact, from conception to completion the whole design took less than a month."

It is a small stroke, but a deft one. Within the limitations of a confined apartment—approximately 1,200 square feet—Billy Gaylord has created an unusual look, quite unrelated to time or place.

"I didn't want anything that could be defined exactly," he says. "The way I arranged the apartment, it could be viable in 1930 or 2001. I designed the furniture myself, and for the rest, chose some striking antiques. I mean I simply didn't use French or English chairs. I wanted something out of the ordinary—like those eighteenth-century African throne chairs in the living room or the Chinese ceremonial chairs in the dining room. By the way, they're far more comfortable than they look!"

Perhaps the major problem he faced in the small apartment is a rather odd oval living room. To the unprofessional eye it might give the impression that the space is quite unlivable.

"Well, it's livable for me," says the designer. "When I come home, I work at the dining room table or read in bed. And I think the oval room is perfect for entertaining. Actually it turns out to be an ideal background for people.

"But I will admit the shape of it presented a good many problems at the beginning. When I first saw the apartment I knew that it needed a lot of help, but I had to work with the oval. There was no way around that, and the whole thing did look like some American idea of a 1930s French hotel suite. I loved it and hated it, if you know what I mean."

The unique space prompted Mr. Gaylord, in spite of an unconscious desire not to take any dramatically positive position, to give free rein to his ingenuity and imagination. He is young, he did not choose to be timid in his design solutions, and the result is a candid flight of fantasy.

In a curious way the fantasy and dramatic thrust of the apartment result almost as much from the dictates of space and economics as from any particular plan on the designer's part. For example, he put quilted padding on the living room wall for soundproofing, largely because it was inexpensive. The padding is simply the same cotton padding moving men use to protect elevators. The only difference is that the padding ordered by the designer is white. Economic factors, too, dictated the enormous banquette covered with pillows, since it was far less costly than buying sofas.

Mr. Gaylord avoids patterns that would make the rooms seem smaller than they are. The background is basically white, clear and simple, to show off paintings, plants, flowers and—most importantly—the people, who, he feels, are the real décor of any effectively designed environment.

The apartment is sparse and objective, with few distractions, but there is a skillful interweaving of strong melodic lines. The oval of the living room,

for instance, is counterpointed by the spiny shape of a large cactus and the jagged layers of a low stone table. The effect, with the simplest and least expensive of ingredients, is theatrical. There is no other word for it, and Mr. Gaylord would be the last to deny such a description. In fact, he is not at all happy to be called an interior designer. He would rather be thought of as an "interior dramatist."

He is pleased with his unusual apartment on Nob Hill, with the simplicity of its concept and the unexpectedly dramatic impact it has. But he has no desire to repeat himself in the future.

"I don't want to do anything expected," he says, "unless it is the unexpected. I want to come up with fresh solutions for each particular design problem. I want clients to tell me how they *really* want to live, not simply what they would like other people to see. I like them to describe favorite rooms, and I go with them to antiques shops and museums and art galleries. And then I go to work."

This is precisely the approach he used for himself in the Nob Hill apartment. He went into seclusion for several weeks and worked out solutions and details in his head. He makes no elaborate preliminary floor plans.

At this early stage in his career, Billy Gaylord has demonstrated in the context of his own apartment a grasp of proportion, clarity, elegance and drama. This understanding is all the more remarkable because the materials he has used are simple and inexpensive, the space limited and awkward.

So his entrance into the design arena on a late afternoon in San Francisco created a degree of enthusiasm that a small apartment by a young new designer does not often generate. Perhaps this is because, in spite of a desire to play it safe, he nevertheless managed, with the freedom of youth, to say something different and provocative.

It was a gesture that managed to impress most favorably the critical and often jaded guests who assembled at the unveiling party. Comments were almost universally laudatory, and at least one guest was heard to remark, "Audacious to be so good at his age." Thus youth and daring—and a limited budget—have any number of advantages.

ABOVE: *The architectural features and small spaces of the uniquely shaped building high on Nob Hill that housed his apartment presented designer Billy Gaylord with a number of intriguing problems.* LEFT: *The ovalness of the Living Room is accentuated by a curving banquette and kidney-shaped table. Because the room is located on a noisy San Francisco corner, Mr. Gaylord covered the walls with sound-muffling fabric quilted in vertical channels and hung from chrome hooks. The spiny cactus and the table formed by a jagged stack of painted flagstone offer dramatic contrast to the room's fluid curves. Art objects include hanging plastic bags by Claes Oldenberg, a box sculpture by Zanne Hochberg and a 17th-century Portuguese statue of St. Ignatius.*

OPPOSITE: *In a view of the Living Room looking through to the dining room/study, the pale walls, bleached wood floors, and pristine flagstone and kidney-shaped tables promote a light, clean background for living things. The pair of African thrones are 18th century.* ABOVE: *A bouquet of vivid tulips provides a lively color note against the achromatic Living Room wall, the banquette and the variously sized pillows.*

OPPOSITE: *The walls of the Dining Room/Study are covered with shirred, bleached canvas held back by chrome hooks at the doorway, effecting a tentlike entrance. The sleek, thick form of the centrally placed dining table/desk contrasts with a pair of lightly scaled and elaborately finished 17th-century Chinese ceremonial chairs. An 18th-* *century mask from Africa is displayed on a canvas-upholstered pedestal.* ABOVE: *Under a canopy of ficus foliage, the shiny white laminated plastic Dining Room table is shown set for two. The classical delicacy of the gilt-edged dinnerware pattern relates to the finely painted details of a pair of deceptively comfortable red-lacquered chairs.*

Mr. Gaylord wanted the Bedroom to be "a quiet peaceful place to wake up to"—a change of pace from the other rooms in his 1,200-square-foot apartment. A large Abstract-Expressionist painting by Zanne Hochberg dominates one wall; the 18th-century Persian chair in front of it came from the former quarters of the Iranian Consulate in San Francisco.

# AN
# ANTIQUES TREASURE
# ENCLAVE

Joseph Rondina is one of those fortunate people whose professional occupations coincide perfectly with their private tastes. Born into a Florentine-American family with a well-established home furnishing business in upstate New York, he inherited an instinctive feeling for furniture and objets d'art, and acquired an early familiarity with the pleasures and perils of interior design.

After graduating from design school, he worked for the family firm as a buyer/decorator. Sixteen years ago, while still in his early twenties, he moved to New York City and started a successful business of his own, buying and selling antique furniture and works of art.

Today his antiques shop on East Sixty-second Street is one of the most attractive examples of its kind, and it enjoys an international reputation. His regular clients include many of the best-known collectors and dealers in Europe and Asia as well as in the United States, and he has exported antiques to no less than nineteen countries. Indicative of the quality of the firm and the character of its owner is the fact that Mr. Rondina's clients have a notable way of becoming close personal friends.

In his shop eighteenth-century French pieces and Oriental antiques—Chinese and Japanese, Korean and Indian, Siamese and Cambodian—vie for attention. In his own apartment they merge and blend unforgettably. The manner in which he juxtaposes all of these cultures gives an impression of extraordinary serenity, and the apartment is reminiscent of certain houses in Paris between the World Wars, where Louis XV and Louis XVI furniture was side by side with ancient Chinese sculpture.

That meeting and mating of the products of different civilizations, which seemed so magical then, no longer surprises. But it still has the power to enchant the senses and satisfy the mind—more especially when, as in Mr. Rondina's apartment, every piece of furniture and every artifact is of the highest quality. And everything has been selected by one who has a love of beauty, a keen intuition and an admiration for fine workmanship.

"I've gradually widened the scope of my aesthetic and antiquarian interests," says Joseph Rondina, "going farther East and deeper into history in search of rare objects."

No doubt all of these exceptional finds are to stock his shop, but they are also for his own use and enjoyment at home. There is no superimposed color scheme, no evidence of sleight of hand with contrasting styles or shapes or textures. Against white walls and off-white floor coverings, with soft beige and subdued blue and muted red in the background, the black of a Chinese screen or the dark green shade of a Louis XVI lamp form dramatic accents. Lacquer and teak, velvet and suede, bronze and porcelain, do the same. The beauty of Mr. Rondina's apartment as a whole is less a result of the sophisticated use of space—or search for effects—than of the emanation of individual concepts.

In the living room, for example, the eye is caught and held by a polychrome carved-wood Sung figure of Kuan-Yin, standing on a Régence commode and backed by a seventeenth-century Korean screen. Nearby, on a gilt table signed by Jacob, are four jars of Ban Chieng pottery, Khmer tomb furnishings recently unearthed in Thailand. In the bedroom a steel and gilt bronze eighteenth-century French bed, upholstered in blue felt and leather, is watched over by a seventeenth-century wooden statue of Vishnu.

In the adjoining dining room—dividing doors have been removed throughout the apartment, so that rooms merge, as well as styles and periods—a twelfth-century Chinese stone Buddha sits cross-legged in meditation on a Régence side table. The sculpture is surrounded by a Ch'ien Lung altar garniture with *blanc de Chine* flasks and K'ang Hsi blue-and-white porcelain on Louis XV gilt brackets on the wall behind.

Here, in the midst of all these treasures, Joseph Rondina likes to entertain his friends when the day's work is over. He is an accomplished cook, adept at preparing not only Italian and French cuisine, but Chinese, Japanese and Korean dishes as well. He lays his table appropriately—with French faïence for Provençal specialties, Peking enamel for Chinese meals, and Japanese ware for Japanese cooking. The relative smallness of his dinner par-ties—normally four, at most six—is also characteristic. For all his success in his profession, and his capacity to make friends easily, he has remained over the years an essentially private person.

"I never give a cocktail party," he says, "nor attend one if I can help it."

He enjoys conversation and can tell a good story. He knows his world and he knows his subject. But he has too keen a sense of the ridiculous to pontificate about his profession or to give a dissertation on his philosophy as an *antiquaire*.

"But I will say," he concedes, "that things I am looking for seem to have an unaccountable way of gravitating in my direction. I'm not above believing that inanimate objects can exert an influence just as surely as people can."

And—who can say?—perhaps the extraordinary serenity of his own apartment has something to do with its complement of Kuan-Yins, Vishnus and Buddhas—merciful, releasing, preserving gods—along with the combination of paintings, both modern and antique (from Artur Bual's contemporary works to seventeenth- century Korean landscape scenes) found in each of the rooms.

Some of Mr. Rondina's colleagues and competitors attribute his success to a knack for keeping abreast of changing fashions. But it would be less parochial to credit him with a rare creative ability to make others share his interest and knowledge in the arts of civilizations remote from our own. He is a fortunate person to have this talent, and a sensitive and positive mind has provided him with an enviably healthy talent for living.

His sensitivity and talent have combined to create a perfect background for the man himself. His apartment is surely not the showcase of a successful antiques dealer. It is, rather, the summary of a lifetime of devotion to beauty and to the acquisition of fine things. There is a hint of philosophy here, in spite of his disclaimers, but it is an unobtrusive kind of philosophy. It is mingled with a gentle humanism and a sense of good taste and good humor. Antiques have little to do with it. The tolerant and understanding approach to life has everything to do with it.

A feeling of power emanates from the art treasures that antiques dealer Joseph Rondina has discerningly assembled in the Living Room of his Manhattan apartment. LEFT: A polychrome carved-wood figure of the Sung Dynasty majestically presides, offset by a Korean painted-silk screen, dated 1605, that depicts an emperor's migration from a winter to a summer palace. Nearby, open-mouthed and menacing, is a 10th-century stone lion from India. Fine European antiques, such as the marble-topped Régence commode, work well with the Oriental pieces. TOP: The collection of Ban Chieng pottery jars—circa 3500 B.C.—are Khmer tomb furnishings that were excavated recently in Thailand. ABOVE: An 18th-century Ch'ien Lung screen and a Khmer sandstone Vishnu create an artistic space division for the adjacent Bedroom.

RIGHT: *A Louis XVI architect's table provides a unique solution for exhibiting art objects in the Bedroom. Appropriately stacked beneath it are four 18th-century tomes on the subject of architecture. Resting on its several surfaces are a small Indian sandstone Vishnu, a Cambodian elephant-shaped jar, a pair of Louis XVI prophyry candlesticks, a pair of 18th-century pistols and an African mask.* BELOW RIGHT: *A 17th-century samurai warrior protects the Dining Room, which is traditionally appointed with a Louis XVI table and armchairs, and a large 18th-century Chinese lacquered cabinet. The table is set for an intimate dinner party, with Chinese porcelain plates and delicate enamel sweetmeat dishes. A Japanese candelabrum provides illumination.*

BELOW: *Louis XVI furnishings—a steel bed upholstered in wool, a bronze guéridon and a gilded bronze lantern—add classical grace to the Bedroom. Two paintings by contemporary Portuguese artist Artur Bual appear to float on a mirrored surface. From a nearby wall a carved figure of Vishnu surveys the room. The linen rug is 19th-century Japanese.*

# AN OUTDOOR SPIRIT

Some rather extensive scene-changing took place in Beverly Hills when Dr. and Mrs. Joseph Pollock supervised an interior restyling of their already special home—for twenty years considered one of California's most interesting.

When such literate and committed clients as the Pollocks choose a literate and committed designer like Kalef Alaton, special things happen. So when Mr. Alaton, of Los Angeles, Istanbul and Paris, made his appearance on the Pollock scene with his associate, Janet Polizzi, a happy fermentation began to develop. Mrs. Pollock was quick to see that Kalef Alaton was able to understand and appreciate her collections of art objects and antique rugs. He saw them, she explains, "not simply as decoration but as art objects."

"We came to know Helene Pollock very well," explains Kalef Alaton. "We saw how she moves in her house, how she sits, talks, entertains. She has great style and is extremely receptive when we present her with an idea."

The decorative changes that arose from this collaboration are evident even on the outside. In a shaded pebble-paved court a quiet wall fountain splashes an accompaniment to masses of blooming potted plants that change color with the seasons. Astoundingly, a rich tomato-red Karabagh runner stretches toward the large entrance doors of the house and gives an immediate preview of the Pollocks' living environment.

Beyond the entrance hall in the house is a long and unusually tall living room. At one end, thirty-foot floor-to-ceiling windows look out across a covered terrace to lush California plantings and a sweeping vista of Los Angeles. There are quantities of antique furniture in the living room, along with a fascinating combination of art objects.

If anything can be said to dominate the redesigned living room, it is the spectacular rug—a hard and pileless Indian durrie, probably made a hundred years ago for the summer palace of some rajah. Its white center field is patterned with rows of large blue elephants in silhouette. In many ways the main emphasis of the room appears to be the floor, and there are stacks of lounging pillows everywhere. But tubs of tall trees and shrubs turn the eye upward, and the art on the walls is impressive: a Nolde watercolor, a Nathan Oliveira oil, and work by Léger, Arp, Craig Kauffman, Ron Davis and Roy Lichtenstein—among others.

Rugs and paintings suggest no matched color scheme and are allowed to exist simply on their own, held together by the owners' love for them and the designer's special magic.

What is the secret of this enchanting room?

"First, I simply looked at it as open space," says Kalef Alaton. "I emptied the room completely so that we could comprehend the size and study it with care. Then I put in the tall trees to emphasize the upward thrust and the scale. Basically it was a question of 'undecorating'—of eliminating all conventional seating arrangements and of opening up the center of the room. We played with color and even with forms the way a painter does, and now I think the room has many different moods and a great deal of flexibility."

"The open center of the room is marvelous for entertaining," says Mrs. Pollock. "It puts people into a very happy frame of mind. There's magic here, and I don't think I can explain it."

Janet Polizzi, a calm counterpoint to Kalef Alaton's intensity, gives a more practical explanation. She points out that in the course of the redesigning many of the rooms had their roles reversed. The dining room has now become a small sitting room, and the old playroom—the Pollock children are all grown—serves as a new, large dining room. Color contributes a good deal to the easy transition from one room to another. For example, the stark white walls of the living room give way to the pale apricot of the sitting room, leading in turn to the Venetian red of the new dining room.

Color thus adds definition to each different space, and the sitting room is, in effect, an extension of the living room as well as a passageway to the dining room. The sitting room is filled with many eclectic pieces: handsome Heriz rugs, comfortable sofas, a French convent table, William and Mary pieces, contemporary paintings and a variety of sculpture—Egyptian, African, pre-Columbian and modern. There is more than a hint of the ornate and the European about the room, and it is exactly the effect Helene Pollock wanted.

"Ten years ago," she explains, "I couldn't have lived in an atmosphere like this. But you develop, as you become interested in art and antiques and study them carefully. Perhaps Europeans understand these things better than we do, because of their long historical background."

Kalef Alaton and Janet Polizzi agree, though with minor reservations: "Working with marvelous things naturally gives the house warmth and perhaps a foreign flavor. But we have not really overdone that aspect. We travel all over the world, and so do the Pollocks. The house could be anywhere—it is thoroughly international."

However, the dining room itself is frankly European, with the rich Venetian red of the painted walls, the Régence sideboard, the lacquered English chairs in the Chippendale style and a collection of candlesticks from the south of France. And Kalef Alaton has added a special contribution in the form of a "Turkish room," a lounge forming a pendant to the dining room. It is a parrot cage of wonders, with Turkish kilims covering the banquettes and on the floor a nomadic Kazak prayer rug with a subtle blue-green field and vigorous geometric borders. Kilim pillows further suggest relaxation and a lingering coffee hour. But the designer is modest in pointing out his contribution to the Pollock house.

"I simply tried to show what could be done in terms of a comfortable California contemporary style. Basically this is a very good house, and I just warmed it up a little."

Mrs. Pollock, on the other hand, is rather more effusive and she is delighted to discuss the effect of the new design: "Yes, we did begin with good architecture and some fine antiques and art. But we added a good interior designer and his associate. The result is that I love the house all over again, just as I did when it was first built.

"Over the years it had become somehow wrong for us. Now it gives me a marvelous lift. What do they say? 'New wine in old bottles'—isn't that the right expression?"

RIGHT: *A vivid Karabagh runner leads majestically toward the entrance to Dr. and Mrs. Joseph Pollock's Beverly Hills residence.* BELOW: *Apricot-colored walls, a Heriz rug and bold Indonesian and French antique fabrics radiate warmth in the comfortable Sitting Room. Artistic elements include exotic African and pre-Columbian objects, a contemporary painting by Lee Mullican and a wall sculpture by Craig Kauffman.* OPPOSITE: *A view of the Living Room reveals an interesting mixture that ranges from the antique to the contemporary. An Indian durrie elephant-motif rug, a Shiraz carpet and a Kermanshah floor pillow enhance the natural-toned tile floor. Other furnishings include hand-carved chairs and a Siamese theatrical makeup trunk.*

The head of a Ming Dynasty Kuan-Yin graces the richly colored Dining Room. Surrounding the table are dining chairs whose Chippendale-style patterned upholstery is augmented by an elaborately designed, deep-toned Bidjar rug. The finely carved Régence sideboard displays a collection of candlesticks; their soft light enhances the abstract forms of a watercolor by Alexander Calder.

LEFT: *The Middle Eastern influence of designers Kalef Alaton and Janet Polizzi is at once apparent on the Patio, which is as enchanting as a Persian garden and reminiscent of the pleasure pavilions mentioned in Middle Eastern poetry. The light, airy space, abundant with plants and flowers, invites quiet relaxation and contemplation. Carved and unfinished wooden furnishings—bent-willow chairs, an 18th-century Portuguese plant-filled cupboard, and an 18th-century English headboard made into a lounge—enrich the natural setting. The cool white walls, floor and upholstery fabrics are accented with a Bokhara rug, antique Tabriz pillows and Persian saddlebag pillows.* BELOW LEFT: *An ornately carved Indian screen and settee provide dramatic accents for the Master Bedroom.*

# A DESIGNER'S NEW IDIOM

"Many of my friends are rich," says interior designer Angelo Donghia. It is a dispassionate observation on the particular circle into which his work plunges him. "They have the means, but few take the time, to pamper themselves."

The designer himself is no sybarite. Hardworking and prolifically creative, he knows the importance of diligence. But a recurrent theme in his outlook is the value of the aesthetic pause.

"The morning is an important part of my life," he says. "I like to open my eyes and know that whatever I do is going to be made easier by an attractive beginning. I like to wake up and see a beautiful flower." There is indeed a Rubrum lily in his elegant black marble bathroom. "Stop to think. What will make you as comfortable as possible? Everything should be arranged, available, attractive. We are indebted to our bathrooms every morning. We need a good mirror, a good light. From here we go on to present ourselves to the world."

He finds peace and reassurance, for example, in such simple and pleasant touches as a fresh piece of starched linen in the drawer that holds his brushes. "Drawer decoration," he explains with a smile.

Angelo Donghia is a major force in interior design today. "He is one of the most original people in the decorating world," says his friend, fashion designer Halston. "He has had a great influence on fabrics. His were the first geometrics of any depth made in America. And he has been very revolutionary in the design of upholstered furniture."

Born in Pennsylvania, Mr. Donghia studied at Middlebury, Columbia and the Parsons School of Design before joining the firm of the late Yale Burge in 1959. He became a partner in 1966, but his productivity was not long confined to interior decorating and furniture design. In 1969 he started & Vice Versa, a fabric house, and has ventured into many other fields as well—from designing sheets to inexpensive lines of furniture.

Nowhere is his energy and independence better illustrated than in the way he has designed his own apartment in New York City's East Seventies. Each room is an example of his desire to make space as pliable and functional as possible.

Over the years his point of view has changed considerably. At one time his tastes ran to the luxurious, to collections of antiques and what he calls "balloony" upholstered pieces. Now, however, he has stripped everything to essentials. Seating is comfortable; accessories are to be used—ashtrays, boxes, vases. Open space is for art, and everything is mobile. The theme is change: Art, furniture and objects can be moved easily from place to place for an endlessly variable environment. And in a larger sense, he wants his duplex apartment to offer the same flexibility to guests and friends as well. It is his wish that they be relaxed, and he has made every effort to amuse them with the unusual, to refresh them with the "aesthetic pause."

"When I ask friends home," he says, "I want them to encounter a nonintimidating form of décor. I want to do something agreeable for people, to bring them as gracefully as possible out of their own worlds and into mine."

When he is entertaining, he will think to do the unorthodox. On a cold winter night, for example, dinner is served in his muted bedroom in front of the blazing fire. His bedroom, of course, is quite unlike the usual sleeping quarters, with its rich cascades of quilted white duck draperies settling softly on a gray velvet carpet. All personal paraphernalia is hidden away in enormous closets. Dinner guests relax on one of a number of puffy gray-flannel-covered pieces: floor pillows, a plump low chaise or a bed that—like all the other furnishings—is Donghia-designed.

He calls it a "movable" room, the only stationary object being the stereo equipment. Everything else can be shifted around with ease. And he particularly enjoys changing the position of the bed according to the season of the year. In winter he rolls it close to the fireplace, and in summer he places it near the French doors that open out over a leafy terrace. A spotlight below casts trellis patterns on the gold ceiling, the sort of effect that delights him.

Although he relishes the ease and mobility of pillowed furniture, the designer has an austere color sense that brings a compensatory hardness to the soft lines of the furniture. Throughout the apartment the basic color scheme is black and white and gray, although the occasional vivid note makes the general restraint all the more effective. In the mirrored entrance hall in summer, for example, he overlays the leopard-patterned staircase carpet with Mexican serapes. The colors vibrate in the cool darkness.

As a completely contemporary designer, he uses antique pieces sparingly but, as with color, to great effect. In an upstairs room composed of white and off-white pieces, he has added an imposing Chinese coromandel screen that he bought from the estate of Coco Chanel. In the large downstairs living room he has punctuated the contemporary décor with a nineteenth-century Japanese bamboo table in a tortoiseshell finish.

He believes in having a balanced relationship with the past. The inherited antique should be kept, he maintains, "not out of some misplaced sense of family loyalty or nostalgia," but because it is beautiful and is cherished in its own right.

"In the future," he explains, "we will have to do without many of the things we once were accustomed to. Fine antiques are rapidly becoming unavailable, and the great craftsmen are disappearing. But at the moment the American market does not seem quite ready for plastics and new materials, although Europeans have accepted them far more readily. Ultimately it will happen here. It will have to happen, even though we have lived through several decades of designers and manufacturers forcing French Provincial on us. But we will have to begin to live more simply.

"My theory has always been that architecture, interior design and fashion itself are determined by political and sociological events. So I see for the immediate future a softer look in all areas of design. I think it's part of a new honesty—a concern with understanding yourself, of being true to yourself."

The message Angelo Donghia wishes to convey is basically a simple one: "You should feel at all times that everything around you is attractive; that *you* are attractive." It is simple advice but, as a glance around his own duplex will confirm, not always easy to execute. It is a tribute to his skill that he has done so with quiet and deceptive simplicity.

The contemporary décor of the downstairs
Living Room expresses Mr. Donghia's utilitarian
design philosophy: Seating is comfortable; all
decorative accessories are functional; and
everything can be moved with minimal effort so
that the room is totally changeable. Antiques are
used sparingly; a lightly scaled 19th-century
Japanese tortoise bamboo table serving as a bar
accents the plump Donghia-designed furniture.
The somewhat austere color scheme—black and
white with a scattering of bright accents—is
modified by the shimmering quality of the walls
and ceiling, and by the abundance of light entering
through undraped windows. The effect is crisp
and clean, grounded in geometric precision yet
relaxed and personalized by casually placed
accoutrements and art works by Richard Giglio,
Mark Strong and Bill Weaver.

In the upstairs Living Room, a Chinese
coromandel screen from Coco Chanel's estate and a
whimsical crystal and glass-beaded chandelier
enrich the modern mode; the Georgian fireplace and
moldings, outlined in white, add architectural
interest. Dark walls and a foil-covered ceiling
harmonize with the light wood floor, simplified
upholstered pieces and African-inspired tables.

In the Master Bedroom, Mr. Donghia shifts
the position of his bed with the seasons. For the
warm summer months, he places it near the French
doors that overlook a verdant garden; when winter
comes, he moves it closer to the fireplace. The
quilted duck draperies and bedcovering, and the
flannel upholstery, amplify the sensuous contours of
the furniture. The painting is by Mark Strong.

# FRENCH PAVILION IN NORTHERN CALIFORNIA

"I wanted a French pavilion," says interior designer Val Arnold. He stretches out his legs and relaxes as he speaks with delight and affection about his country home in northern California.

What he has created on a small scale is indeed a pleasure pavilion, much like those that flourished around Versailles in the eighteenth century. Such retreats provided an escape from the pressures and intrigues of court life. In a sense, Mr. Arnold wished to provide the same sort of retreat for himself.

"Today in America," he says, "there are even more pressures. There is the stress factor and the economic factor; the complete mobility of society and the many demands on the individual. It is more necessary than ever for a person to have a place in which to relax—to have a true change in environment once in a while, a complete degree of privacy."

The need for relaxation and privacy are particularly compelling in his own circumstances, since his home in San Francisco occupies the same building as his office. It is therapeutic for him to close the door on these responsibilities occasionally.

"But I'm not a very good traveler," he comments. "I travel only when I have to, but I've always managed to have a place in the country. And I think the relaxation and change of pace you get from weekends in the country are more important in the long run, and more worthwhile, than long vacations and traveling far distances."

For about five years Mr. Arnold had rented a weekend retreat on the beach in Marin County, across the Golden Gate Bridge from San Francisco. When the owners moved back he decided that the time had come for him to buy a house for himself. It happened that some years before, he had heard about an interesting small house near Santa Rosa, some fifty miles north of San Francisco.

It had been built as a summer home, Mr. Arnold explains, "by a man whose taste I respect very much." But at a later date it was acquired by another owner who, unfortunately, rented it to careless and neglectful tenants.

"When I went up to see it for the first time," the designer recalls, "it was raining, and the whole place looked something like *Tara* after the Civil War. There were broken bottles everywhere, and piles of old newspapers. All the rooms were unbelievably crammed with junk. To top it off, about thirty cats were living in the house. It was all very depressing, and I was discouraged. But I could see that fortunately the basic house was still there."

In any event, he went ahead and bought it. The house was a relatively small structure with no bedroom. It did, however, have a garden house, two beautiful allées of trees and a small pool.

"At first I thought I could live very comfortably in the main house," says Mr. Arnold, "and use the house in the back, which was not finished, as a garden and maintenance room. But after I was there for a while, I saw that the arrangement wasn't very satisfactory. It didn't give me much privacy, and of course I had to have a bedroom. As a matter of fact, I once lived in a house that had the bedroom in a separate building; I remember I liked the idea, so I decided that I would use it here."

So the garden house was transformed into the bedroom. And the more Val Arnold worked with the structure, the more impressed he was with the beauty of its original design.

"One day I was looking through a book about famous old houses in France," he says, "and I began to see parts of my own house in it. There were many beautiful details, and I was particularly anxious to keep the original architectural feeling. It's a slow process. You have to understand what a house is, before you can develop it in any satisfactory way."

Having adapted the second structure to house his bedroom, he turned the pool flanking the two buildings into a lily pond, balanced ecologically and stocked with Japanese carp. At a short distance from this complex he added a larger pool, and then he concentrated on the landscaping.

"Peter Logan spent three years landscaping the area," he says. "He kept everything very rural. The project turned out to be fantastically expensive, because we planted full-grown trees and put in a lawn, with a sprinkling system. But it was worth it in the long run. In the springtime there are thousands and thousands of daffodils, and all year round

there's always something to use indoors."

The house expands gracefully into the surrounding area. During the summer months the designer and his friends are inclined to "live outside," able to enjoy the pleasure from May through October and sometimes until the end of November. The pool—"Nothing like a city pool, with a patio or terrace,"says Mr. Arnold—is situated in the middle of a meadow, and the complex of houses can be seen reflected on its surface. Water is filtered and recycled through a special process used by astronauts on space trips. Again, maintenance is almost nonexistent, since the pool is heated by solar panels carefully hidden behind the trees.

Thus the small estate has, in Mr. Arnold's words, "all the visual benefits of country living, with few of the problems." In the valley below lies an eighty-five-acre dairy preserve, and the view of a rare pastoral scene of cows, horses and sheep is conveniently there to be admired, but not maintained, by Mr. Arnold.

With a high bluff on one side of the property, a ravine on another and trees all around, there is little likelihood that the view will ever change. But in order to ensure seclusion, the owner added two acres to his property several years ago.

"It's an exciting house for me," says Mr. Arnold, with obvious pleasure. "The rooms are perfectly proportioned, with a minimum of openings and a generous feeling of space. I wanted the house to be picturesque—and I think it is. But at the same time, I wanted it to be cozy and comfortable and—to be honest—luxurious."

The house is also practical—there are two dogs, two cats and even an occasional bird in residence. Décor is simple and easy to maintain: tile floors, sisal matting and lots of baskets. The generous array of baskets, in fact, is put to frequent use by the designer and his guests during the summer, for picnics under the trees.

In the summertime, when there are many guests, white canvas slip covers and matting hold sway. But winter is the time for a blazing fire.

"My little pavilion was a labor of love," says Val Arnold. "It's part of me now."

ABOVE: *A tranquil, tree-lined allée leads to the Main House of designer Val Arnold's weekend oasis in the wine country of northern California.* RIGHT: *Mr. Arnold transformed the spatial limitations imposed by a small main structure into an asset by converting a garden house into a Master Bedroom Suite that resembles a French pavilion. His bedroom overlooks a peaceful lily pond filled with Japanese carp.*

Color unifies the well-proportioned Living Room,
whose walls blend easily with the terra-cotta floor.
A muted variant of the same color, in velvet,
has been used to upholster the deep-cushioned sofa
and chairs and built-in window seat, while the
durrie rug is a still lighter shade of the same hue.
Blue-and-white porcelains distributed throughout
the room provide a consistent series of accents.

*Further Living Room views:* BELOW: *Surveying the scene from her perch on the mantel is an 18th-century French carved-wood sphinx.* BELOW RIGHT: *A burst of colorful flowers seems even more vivid next to the limited palate of Oriental blue-and-white porcelain objects.* LOWER: *A Georgian-style shade endows the bay window and window seat with a prosceniumlike quality.*

Texture predominates in the Master Bedroom, where the walls have a heavy raked-paint finish and the floorcovering is of sisal matting. The soft cotton covering the bed and the pair of channeled lounge chairs is particularly inviting. A painting by Michael Dailey, an Indian pot and a Philippine carved angel are among the few, carefully chosen decorative objects.

LEFT: *A pleasant work area is provided by a desk placed in a quiet corner of the Kitchen overlooking the courtyard. The intricately carved desk chair is from Burma. As in the living room, the floor has been covered with terra-cotta tile; but here, small blue-and-white tiles have been added. A profusion of plants placed near the window obscures the dividing line between indoors and outdoors, making the presence of the countryside still more dominant.* BELOW: *With 6½ acres and many shady glades to choose from, there is no lack of picnic spots on the small estate. A convenient way to carry lunch is in some of the many baskets that Val Arnold has collected. When not commandeered for picnics, these baskets double as decorative elements throughout the house.*

# VISTA
# OF THE
# PACIFIC OCEAN

In spite of innumerable other claims, it has long been established that the most equable climate in southern California is to be found in San Diego and such neighboring towns as La Jolla and Del Mar, San Clemente and San Juan Capistrano.

As well as having a climate almost impossible to duplicate in any other part of the United States, perhaps in the world, the area around San Diego is particularly rich in the early history of the country. Everywhere there are traces of the Spanish settlers, the Mexican governors and the first Californians themselves. Spanish missions, founded by Father Junipero Serra on his painful journey north, still stand at intervals along the *Camino Real* all the way to San Francisco, and the course of the great "royal road" is followed today. The coastal areas are renowned for dramatic cliffs and beaches and the evocative expanse of the Pacific Ocean—carrying the imagination to the Hawaiian Islands, to China and Japan, to all the exotic ports of the Far East.

In 1938 these compelling factors brought Mr. and Mrs. William Hall Tippett from Oklahoma City to southern California, to find some appropriate property for themselves. Mrs. Tippett recalls that her late husband went so far as to contact Washington, D.C., to find out which part of the country was considered to have the best climate. The answer was definitive: Del Mar, California. And here they found five acres in a dramatic and unparalleled setting, eighty feet above the beach, fronting the endless vista of the Pacific Ocean.

"The location was, and is, magnificent," says Mrs. Tippett. "But when I look at *Tippett Hall* today, it's hard for me to remember that in 1938 there was nothing here but a bare field—no trees, no flowers, nothing." Today there are landscaped gardens, flowering peach trees, thousands of hydrangeas—breathtaking at their prime, in August—Monterey cypresses, stone pines from Presidio Park, and enormous palm trees, which were started in small pots and now tower over the great expanse of green lawn leading to the cliff's edge.

"The soil here is like chocolate cake," says Mrs. Tippett, and she attributes much of the success of her present gardens to the original work done by landscape designer Paul Avery, as well as to continual care by a staff of gardeners.

From the beginning, the entire project was in Ruth Tippett's hands, since her husband had said, in no uncertain terms, "It's up to you." Quite undaunted by the challenge, she called first upon the services of Pasadena architect Robert Farquhar to create the kind of house she and her husband wanted. She had been educated in the South, Mr. Tippett came from Kentucky, and there was no conflict about the form the house would take. It was to be Georgian, with definite echoes of a true southern plantation house.

"And naturally we had to have magnolias," says Mrs. Tippett. "You can't have this kind of house without them, can you?"

The design and construction of the Georgian-style house took the best part of a year, and it was built in a way, and with a sense of devotion, not often encountered today. Swedish craftsmen from Pasadena were responsible for most of the work on the wooden structure. They used only seasoned wood, and there are architectural details that perhaps will never be duplicated again. One particular craftsman, Mrs. Tippett remembers, was in charge of building the staircase for the central hall. She told him she wanted to make certain that none of the steps would squeak.

"Simple enough," he said. "Just get me a sack of Bermuda onions."

The staircase arrived, unassembled, and Mrs. Tippett watched in amazement as the craftsman rubbed each part with onion juice before it was glued and set into place. This unique treatment accomplished its purpose—from that day, the stairs have never squeaked.

Such care and devotion to detail are quite as characteristic of the interiors of the house—interiors entirely planned and arranged by Ruth Tippett herself. She had long been interested in décor, and while traveling abroad on concert tours she had devoted much of her free time to antiques shops, furniture galleries and fabric houses. Now there was an entire house to fill, and she approached the problem in an efficient and professional way. After consulting the architect's plans, she made a careful diagram of each of the rooms. These diagrams allowed her to arrange the décor and to work out color schemes long before she acquired the antiques and furniture and fabrics she wanted.

"Everything was planned ahead of time," she explains. "In the long run, I think it made everything very much easier. I carried cards based on the architect's plan for each room with me—to the showrooms of New York and Chicago, but mostly to Europe. I found much of the furniture in France and a great deal else in Italy. Most of the glassware, for example, and practically all of the chandeliers come from Venice, and the fabrics were made in Florence. There are also some wonderful old statues from Italy in the garden. The larger ones, representing the four seasons, arrived wrapped up like mummies, in what I can only describe as coffins. I had no idea how to deal with them, and I called Forest Lawn Cemetery for advice. They sent a man down here, and he stayed three days, putting the statues in the proper setting. They're still positioned exactly where he placed them."

Tippett Hall stands today almost exactly as it was conceived some forty years ago. With its generous verandas in the southern manner, its great lawn sweeping toward the sea, and its towering palms and cypresses, the house possesses a magic aura of peace, tranquillity and gracious hospitality. It is not for decoration alone that the traditional pineapple of welcome is carved on the exterior of Tippett Hall.

And it is by no means a paradox to find what is essentially a southern plantation house in an area of southern California rich with echoes of the Spanish Colonial period. Though separated by centuries, graciousness and hospitality were characteristic of both cultures—cultures concerned with an unhurried and comfortable way of life. The family and the home were of primary importance. Tippett Hall is sufficiently grand, to be sure, but above everything else, it has been, and it is, a home.

"My husband and I never thought of the house as a showplace of any kind," says Mrs. Tippett. "It was our home, built with love—and I hope it will be here for a hundred years."

Tippet Hall, *a large white clapboard Georgian-style manor house at Del Mar, California, is reminiscent of a southern plantation. Designed by Pasadena architect Robert Farquhar, it was built for Mr. and Mrs. William Hall Tippet in 1938 on a dramatic five-acre site overlooking the Pacific Ocean. The design and the exacting construction, which was accomplished by a crew of Swedish craftsmen, took almost a year to complete. Assisted by landscape designer Paul Avery, Ruth Tippett undertook the taming of the windswept, barren hilltop; the acreage was planted to rolling lawns, tall pines and magnolias, and a profusion of pink hydrangeas. Having benefited from years of devoted attention and the gentle climate of Del Mar, the landscape has been transformed into formal and informal gardens of outstanding natural beauty.*

To encourage a feeling of Old World elegance
in the Drawing Room, Mrs. Tippett chose a cut-
velvet wallcovering, draperies with Italian silk
tassel fringe and Brussels lace undercurtains, and
a pair of Venetian amber-glass chandeliers. She
purchased many of the furnishings and objets
d'art—primarily 18th-century French—during
frequent trips to Europe for operatic engagements.

BELOW: *The view of the Formal Garden from a second-story window reveals a lily pond surrounded by concentric circles of meticulously clipped boxwood hedges and unusual varieties of rose bushes. Pathways radiating from the tranquil pond lead through miniature Colonial-style gates to informal gardens and woodland trails that are also part of the Tippett acreage.*

OPPOSITE: *A 17th-century carving attributed to Grinling Gibbons of wheat and a shell—symbolizing land and sea—ornaments the overdoor between the living room and the Dining Room. Antique scenic wallpaper by Zuber depicts the Seven Wonders of the World. Chippendale-style chairs surround an expandable table set with Venetian lace and crystal, Tiffany plates and a Georgian silver epergne. Glistening overhead is a French chandelier of rock crystal and ormolu.*

# THEME

# OF

# ANTIQUITY

"Certainly it was the view," says interior designer William Chidester emphatically. "I know that doesn't sound very original, but it's the reason I bought the property and built the house. I knew I had to take advantage of this fine view."

To say the view is merely "fine" is an understatement. It is spectacular, and the site on which Mr. Chidester chose to build his new house is one of the most captivating in the Los Angeles area.

High in the hills north of Sunset Boulevard, the house commands an almost 180-degree panorama of the vast city below. During the day the view stretches all the way from the San Gabriel Mountains to the Pacific Ocean, and at night the million lights of the city sparkle below like diamonds on a background of black velvet.

Architect Walter Wilkman, in consultation with Mr. Chidester, was careful to make certain that almost every room in the new house enjoyed the panoramic view. To this end a U-shaped house was designed around a small swimming pool. The living room and dining room were placed at the bottom of the U, and bedroom suites occupy each end. At night, in particular, the interesting effect calls to mind the interior of an airplane making some eternal approach to Los Angeles.

For these obvious reasons Mr. Chidester is inclined to emphasize the view and credit the architect with the impact the house has. But the contributions he himself has made as interior designer are of equal importance. The house is not large—some 4,500 square feet—but the interiors have been cleverly arranged to complement all the opulence and grandeur of the view, and in their own way they are equally grand. There is an overwhelming natural beauty outside, and William Chidester has maintained the same atmosphere, albeit in miniature, within the house itself.

Consequently, the theme of the interior design is one of opulence, and the space is arranged to suggest the infinite vistas outside. Ceilings in the living room and in the gallery are thirteen feet high, and those in the rest of the house are ten feet high. The drama of the setting calls for an equivalent drama within, and the designer has provided this with a lavish hand. The fact that he has his own showroom and antiques shop helped considerably. In such a way he gathered some of the rich materials with which to create the interiors of his house.

"When you have a shop," he explains, "you are inevitably going to find yourself with a surplus of everything. The fact is that for each new design project I undertook, I had to go out and buy different antiques and different accessories.

"The people I was working for had other effects in mind; they wanted other things, and naturally it was my responsibility to satisfy their wishes. So, for a number of years, I've had a great many marvelous objects left over. In terms of this new house it was a very fortunate circumstance."

It is something of a truism that interior designers do not often do their best work for themselves. Inevitably some of them lose the proper perspective, since what they are doing is so personal. William Chidester, on the other hand, by taking advantage of the antiques and rare furnishings collected for himself and his shop over the years, avoided the loss of perspective entirely. His taste had been molded, and he knew instinctively what form his house would take.

Within what is basically a small context, he arranged the interiors to suggest more than a hint of the palatial. And the richness of individual pieces contributes to the overall effect: Louis XV marble mantels, handsome Oushak rugs, parquet flooring, Venetian mirrors, antique torchères, and here and there on tabletops a generous mixture of objects from almost every period. Furniture ranges from French Directoire to Italian Provincial and Irish Regency, and luxurious fabrics complete the impression of grandeur and European opulence.

In the living room, an unusual mural by Douglas Riseborough sets the tone of the interior design more precisely than anything else. Though it does not appear to be, the mural is modern—acrylic on canvas. The center panel, a view of Marrakech, was painted in 1962, finding a place of honor in Mr. Chidester's previous home. In the new house the canvas was transferred to a larger wall, and the artist added side panels and trompe l'oeil figures—the

whole suggesting nothing so much as a room in the Doge's Palace in Venice. It is a lush fantasy that emphasizes and repeats the opulent antiques and furnishings the designer has meticulously chosen for the new interiors. A logical question concerns the significance that a scene of Marrakech would have for Mr. Chidester.

"None at all," the designer says with a smile. "Originally the artist asked me what I would like him to paint, and I said it was entirely up to him. At that time, back in 1962, he had just returned from a holiday in North Africa. So here it is."

Yet, if there is no literal meaning in the mural for Mr. Chidester, there is surely a symbolic one. In a curious way, particularly with the addition of the new panels required for a larger wall, the mural is at once the focus and the definition of the interiors. Realistic and fanciful at the same time, it is as much in keeping with the décor as it is with the magnificent natural setting of the house. The painting, the interior design and the locale itself—all are bold strokes; all are on the edge of the overpowering. In amateur hands the result would surely be ostentation, but William Chidester has exercised the most careful control. He has been able to find, almost unconsciously, the perfect expression of his own tastes, and to arrange the background—Rococo as it may be—in a way that makes him entirely comfortable. He envisioned the look he wanted, and then developed it in an almost spontaneous way.

"I had only myself to consult," he is delighted to explain. "That makes a very great difference. When I do a house for clients, on the other hand, I make a complete plan, which we go over at length. It's the only proper thing to do, since the design must reflect their ideas and their way of life. But for my own home, my individual taste and preferences were the only considerations."

And he has made a personal expression, without the lack of certainty that sometimes accompanies the work an interior designer does for himself. With a sure touch, he has accomplished what he set out to do at the beginning: to create a house that complements in full measure one of the more spectacular sites in southern California.

The Living Room of designer William Chidester's Los Angeles hillside residence is a dramatic mélange evocative of faraway times and places. Artist Douglas Riseborough created the monumental trompe l'oeil mural— a scene of Marrakech stylistically reminiscent of Italian Baroque painting. With such a theatrical element as a backdrop, Mr. Chidester chose an assemblage of ornate furnishings, objets d'art and luxurious fabrics to enrich the amply proportioned room. The chandelier and a pair of glass-topped tables resting on the Oushak rug were made from parts of antique torchères. The 13-foot-high ceiling beams are painted in colors that echo and balance the powerful mural.

The distinctive Living Room floor is basketweave-patterned oak parquet with dark-stained borders. Small figures of animals and birds, along with leopard-patterned calfskin covering a Régence chair and cushions, extend the abundance of natural imagery. A contemporary sofa takes on an Old World quality with the addition of tasseled fringe to its base.

Visible from this angle is the terrace adjoining the Living Room and separated from it by sliding glass doors that disappear into the walls. When the doors are open, the treillaged area becomes an outdoor extension of the room. The view also reveals a corner dominated by a scroll-topped armoire; before it is a Chinese drum table—an appropriate perch for a Chinese porcelain bird.

OPPOSITE: *Beyond the living room, the treillage-covered Terrace and the illuminated swimming pool is the spectacular panoramic view that impelled Mr. Chidester to choose this site. The U-shaped structure he built takes full advantage of a 180-degree vista, with bedroom suites located at each end of the U. Twinkling city lights and the contemporary architecture update the antique look of the interiors.*

# MASTERY
# OF VERTICAL
# SPACE

His relative youthfulness notwithstanding, Arthur Smith might justifiably claim to be among the better-known interior designers working in New York City. The fact that he would not dream of making such a claim is irrelevant, except as an indication of two of the qualities responsible for his success: good manners and good sense.

In the contemporary world of art and fashion there is a temptation for those moving up to suggest that they sprang like Minerva, fully armed, from Jupiter's head. Here is one person at least who insists on outlining his debt to those who taught and guided him during his apprenticeship.

Born in Georgia, Mr. Smith studied for five years at the School of Architecture of the University of Auburn, in Alabama—one year of industrial design and four years of interior design. In retrospect he regards that first year in particular as an invaluable learning experience.

"It has enabled me to see at once when something is wrong with proportions," he explains.

Visiting New York while still a student, he was admonished by a gifted Atlanta designer, the late Charles Townsend, to look and look again at the collections in the Metropolitan and Frick museums.

"And that," says Mr. Smith, "was how I started to think for myself about the history of design, and learned everything I could about the past."

When he moved to New York City in the mid-1960s, he found work with the late Edward Garratt, a well-known antiques dealer, from whom he received further training in the history of design. Eight months later he was offered, and accepted, the position of assistant to Billy Baldwin in the design firm of Baldwin & Martin.

Billy Baldwin had been looking for someone not previously trained by another interior designer. Arthur Smith filled the bill and struck Mr. Baldwin as a young man of notable ability, with a useful architectural background as well as a sure sense of color and composition.

"Send them out to get samples," says Billy Baldwin, describing his teaching technique with trainees. "That's how you learn whether they have natural taste. Arthur never brought back things I didn't like. He caught on quickly, but he never accepted anything blindly. He had to be persuaded, and he still battles with clients—as he used to battle with me—about what is best."

For his part, Arthur Smith, after recalling all that Billy Baldwin had to offer an assistant—including the delight of working and traveling with one who happens to be excellent company—sums it up in the following way: "He shortened my formative experience immensely. Anyone else would have taken three times as long."

In 1971 the assistant became a partner in the firm. And in 1973, when Billy Baldwin retired and the firm came to an end, the new firm of Arthur E. Smith took its place. It occupied the same attractive premises, employed the same secretary, bookkeeper and receptionist—and reserved an office with a desk and telephone for Mr. Baldwin, in the event that he should feel nostalgic.

The professional work of the one-time pupil has much in common with that of the one-time mentor: neatness, elegance, simplicity, a clean look. Despite the debt he acknowledges to Mr. Baldwin, Mr. Smith is anything but an imitator. The decorating idiom he has developed over the years is resolutely and unmistakably his own.

His duplex on the top two floors of a house in the East Seventies in New York City is a good example. Windows look over a pleasant terrace onto gardens, and there are few high-rise buildings within close range. The first effect of the apartment seems somber; the entrance hall has black walls and so has the adjoining bedroom. Following suit, the kitchen, too, is almost totally black.

But the undeniable fact is that there is nothing remotely austere or claustrophobic about any of the rooms. Paradoxically enough, the black walls of the hall, bedroom and kitchen create an illusion of unlimited space. Everywhere the contrasts of black and white—some violent, others gently subtle—recall the truism that black-and-white photographs are often incomparably warmer and more sensuous than the most brilliant color transparencies. The living room, in particular, provides an admirable example of the way color—even what might be called noncolor—has of satisfying the eye when allied with intelligent design.

Although Arthur Smith refers to himself invariably as an *interior decorator*, he is actually a more authentic interior designer than many others who are in the habit of using the currently more fashionable term. For example, rather than make his clients buy costly and impressive antiques in the interests of filling space, he prefers to design furniture for them, to fit their individual needs and tastes as well as the particular spatial scheme.

Since many of today's interiors tend to have a more temporary existence than the interiors of the past, he often designs easily movable and portable furniture. He has already designed more than twenty different kinds of lamps. For his own apartment, he designed the bed and chest of drawers in the bedroom, the long wall cabinet with a travertine top in the living room—for television, storage and stereo speakers—and all the geometrically patterned carpets in the bedroom and hall.

Of Arthur Smith's carpet designs Billy Baldwin himself remarks: "Arthur's carpets lie down. They don't stand up and hit you in the face."

Subtlety is Mr. Smith's particular hallmark, and it is evident everywhere in his small and attractive duplex. In trying to define the essential quality of the apartment, and his own particular approach to design—with its blend of restraint and boldness, its contemporary vigor and traditional good sense—the advice of the French philosopher Alain to those of his students who aspired to write comes easily to mind: "Memory is a form of prophecy. First, continue; and then, begin."

The theme of continuity is one that is well understood by Mr. Smith, and evident even within the small confines of his New York apartment—evident, perhaps more particularly, in terms of what appears to be an essentially contemporary statement. It is only those who have studied the past with care and affection who can advance into the future and see, in the case of one in his profession, the historical continuity of design—like the artist, who must learn the realities of anatomy before he can indulge in the imaginary strokes of the abstract.

ABOVE LEFT: *A 1st-century Roman sculpture interjects a classical note into the contemporary Living Room of designer Arthur Smith's Manhattan duplex apartment. A mirrored wall compresses two thousand years into a single image by reflecting a superimposition of the Roman figure onto a 1974 canvas by Al Held.* ABOVE: *Walls covered in brown wrapping paper are a neutral foil for the powerful Ellsworth Kelly canvas that dominates the staircase landing.* OPPOSITE: *Al Held's diagrammatic* Solar Wind VI *establishes geometry as the organizing principle of the Living Room, in which sofa cushions and an Moroccan rug are grids built on the diagonal.*

OPPOSITE: *An elevated perspective reveals the clean simplicity of the Living Room. Beneath the mirrored wall is a low travertine-topped cabinet designed by Mr. Smith to provide storage space for television and stereo equipment, and a suitable surface for exhibiting works of art. Chairs upholstered in white fabric woven with black squares echo the Held painting and conform to the geometric patterns of the sofa cushions and rug. Sisal matting repeats the natural tone of the walls.*

*Black-lacquered walls in the Bedroom are a dramatic backdrop for chiaroscuro works of art.*
ABOVE: *A diamond-shaped canvas by Bolotowsky and two drawings by Franz Kline illuminate the area surrounding the upholstered bed. The carpet sparkles like a sky full of orderly stars, while continuing the geometric patterning of the living room.* ABOVE RIGHT: *Sculptures by Stephen Porter converge beneath a Hantai painting.*

# REFRESHING SETTING IN THE CITY

It is something of a cliché that, in spite of the work of all the interior designers in the world, a house persists in reflecting the personality and taste of its owner. And in those cases where the design bears the unmistakable signature and spirit of its professional author, even more is revealed about the owner. Sometimes, in fact, the very lack of owner interest appears to cry out from every corner, and the most perfectly finished result has no apparent meaning.

This is certainly not the case in the matter of the interiors designed by John Cottrell for the Beverly Hills house of Ingrid Ohrbach, now Mrs. Arthur Ryan. If all the fabrics had her monogram on them the house could not reflect the impact of her personality more clearly. The lady herself is a blue-eyed Scandinavian beauty, and this fact alone called for the use of a light palette and a graceful touch. Mr. Cottrell succeeded in creating the felicitous setting necessary— a setting that has worked well for the owner, reflecting her interest in, and concern for, style and her airy springtime tastes.

The designer looks back on the project with delight, emphasizing the excellent working relationship he had with Mrs. Ryan. The house in the non-hilly part of Beverly Hills was rather unusual in one respect: At that time Mrs. Ryan's permanent residence was a spacious house north of Malibu, with a tennis court near the beach and ample room for weekend guests. But she had conceived the idea of having, in addition, a small and attractive house in town. It was to be in some convenient location, to serve as a weekday retreat and a respite from driving the great southern California distances.

To this end she chose a location in Beverly Hills, convenient to shops and restaurants and theaters. The house itself required hardly any structural changes, and with the collaboration of designer Cottrell it soon became exactly what she had in mind: a pied-à-terre in a lovely garden setting with few maintenance problems.

Seen from the street, the exterior façade is simple and unpretentious. But there is a preview of the eternal springtime atmosphere of the newly completed interiors in the pair of generous fruit trees in terra-cotta pots flanking the entrance door.

The trees are changed with the seasons, and whether they bear lemons, oranges, tangerines or limes, they are always lush and full—presenting a colorful welcome to the fortunate visitor.

Beyond the entrance hall the living room seems to flow effortlessly in the direction of the lanai and pool. This charming vista encompasses an indoor garden of cheerful floral prints on comfortable oversized sofas punctuated by tall, graceful *Ficus benjamina.* The bursts of color suggest nothing so much as a giant spring bouquet of flowers—again an example of the owner's personality.

With only one bedroom, the house is small, but the designer has succeeded in suggesting a generous feeling of space throughout. The effect was not difficult to achieve, since tall doors in the living room and the dining room open to the lanai and the outdoors. With little sleight of hand involved, the house manages to appear a good deal larger than it really is.

Perhaps another reason is that Mr. Cottrell's selection of fabrics almost literally turned the interiors into a spacious garden. In fact, the only decidedly indoor room in the house is a small library off the entrance hall. It is a quiet pine-paneled retreat—the sort of hushed room, in fact, where one would expect to go over important papers with the family lawyer. A handsome antique French commode conceals a seldom-used television set, and there are some fine examples of contemporary art on the walls. But paintings and sculptures and other objects are moved regularly, since Mrs. Ryan is a collector who loves to change and add with regularity. Such casual flexibility enhances the considerable charm and informality of the house.

The owner has friends all over the world, and she enjoys traveling a good portion of the year. For this reason it was necessary that her Beverly Hills retreat be easily maintained, opened and closed at a moment's notice. But the wish for easy maintenance presented the designer with some problems, since Mrs. Ryan entertains extensively. John Cottrell saw to it that the cozy oval dining room table could easily expand to accommodate as many as fourteen dinner guests. And in order to honor the owner's

concept of a daily scene that could be readily changed, he provided a variety of slipcovers for upholstered pieces. Thus, many different moods and effects can be created, depending upon the type of party she wishes to give.

No doubt because of her Scandinavian heritage, flowers and plants seem to mean more to Mrs. Ryan than they do to the average Californian, who tends to take them for granted. Since the fabrics used throughout the house seem to include all the colors of a garden, she enjoys filling the rooms with dominant flowers at their seasonal best: pink azaleas or yellow tulips or daffodils. And pots of cymbidiums, as well as orchids of the more obscure varieties, constantly embellish the rooms with rich, colorful and natural accents.

"Ingrid is an ideal person for whom to design," says John Cottrell. "She is as fresh as a spring breeze, but there is no nonsense about her. She is able to make a decision and stick to it. Hemming and hawing are unknown to her, and because of her devotion to change and development she never wants anything particularly complicated or impractical around. So we used cottons and linens throughout the house, and the living room floor is covered with simple sisal matting."

The designer also is able to make a decision and keep to it, and he takes great pride in setting an installation date for his work—and meeting it. How he can do it in this day and age is something of a mystery, but he established such a date for the completion of Mrs. Ryan's Beverly Hills house—and suggested she take the occasion to arrange a party.

With full confidence she summoned her favorite friends, ordered champagne and arrived herself at the appointed hour with four black limousines filled with clothes. John Cottrell was as good as his word: The house was finished exactly on time and it fulfilled all of her expectations. Every detail promised comfort and convenience, and shone with her own springtime tastes.

From the beginning the designer had understood that a most personal feminine statement was necessary for Mrs. Ryan's city retreat—and he provided it punctually and exactly.

OPPOSITE: *Reflections in the swimming pool at the Beverly Hills home of Mrs. Arthur Ryan restate the tropical splendor of the spacious Lanai, which can be enclosed by clear plastic shades stored in its tentlike top. The interior of the house seems to flow through to the outside; sliding glass doors open to the master bedroom, living and dining rooms. The sofa and chairs are upholstered wicker.*

*Flowers and plants play important roles; since all the colors of the garden appear in the Living Room, Mrs. Ryan can change the dominant tone of the room with masses of pink azaleas, yellow tulips, daffodils or other flora at its seasonal best. Tall graceful Ficus benjamina and a garland of azaleas repeat in reality the floral print of the inviting sofa. Both architecture and furnishings are distinctly functional and uncluttered. The floor is covered with simple sisal matting.*

*The color scheme of the Dining Room enhances a Chinese Export porcelain collection. A mirrored wall adds dimension, as does the accessibility to the lanai past latticework folding doors. The Louis XIII-style dining table is expandable and the high-backed chairs have changeable slipcovers for variety of mood.*

OPPOSITE: *An airy document print turns the Master Bedroom into an idyllic bower. Blossoming branches and flowering plants augment the springlike effect. Covering the draped bed are matching comforter and ruffled pillow shams; a Louis XV chinoiserie lacquered desk adds an antique note. The parquet flooring is covered with a geometrically patterned linen and wool rug.*

ABOVE: *Another view of the breezy Lanai exhibits the privacy of its high-walled garden setting and capacious 60-by-18-foot size—perfect for large-scale entertaining. The neutral tones and natural shades of sisal matting, wicker and bamboo furnishings, and canvas upholstery promote cool informality and ease of maintenance. Patterned cushions, Oriental pottery garden stools and dining table accessories add lively color accents.*

# AN EVENING
# MOOD
# DEFINED

Interior designer Melvin Dwork has his origins, as so many New Yorkers do, in the Midwest. He comes, in fact, from Kansas City, an area noted for a particular kind of quiet sophistication and understated elegance. These qualities are clearly reflected in his character and naturally set the mood for his design concepts, concepts that seem quite at home in any environment where comfort and personal expression are the criteria for good taste.

For this reason there have been many people more than pleased with Mr. Dwork's work, and there is one person in particular for whom he has successfully completed at least three designs: a country house, an office and a Manhattan apartment. The relationship has lasted for more than fifteen years, and a recent project is a floor-through apartment in an elegant New York townhouse.

"The owner basically wanted an updated version of his country house," says the designer. "He had turned his personal interests more in the direction of contemporary design."

This change of direction was a happy one for Mr. Dwork. The décor of the country house had been created largely in an eighteenth-century French and English genre, since the designer naturally respected the owner's wishes. His own tastes, however, were rather more contemporary, and he is most pleased now that the owner of the country house decided to move in that direction when it came time to design his New York apartment.

Although the apartment is rented, Melvin Dwork undertook some major structural changes. He kept the fine proportions of the long entrance hall and the spacious front living room, but he combined two smaller rooms in the back to make a large bed/sitting room. He remodeled the bathroom—formerly there had been two—and considerably modernized the kitchen.

The key color is a rich aubergine—a color, incidentally, that the designer had used with great success for his client's office. It is a difficult color to use, but Mr. Dwork made certain that the shade chosen for the apartment was warm and flattering for residents and visitors alike. The color seems to change hourly with the light, both natural and artificial, and it gives depth and subtlety to what is essentially a traditional spatial arrangement.

Since the designer is himself architecturally oriented, he pays a good deal of attention to the use of space. The creation of form with light and color is merely one of the ways in which he handles the problem. Actually there is something of a feeling of mystery in the way he manipulates space through the careful balance and interplay of light and dark areas. The mystery is essentially structural, since the designer has succeeded in making the space seem larger than it really is, and rooms appear to have no beginning and no end. One area flows smoothly into another, and the entire space appears to the eye as a harmonious totality. Space is extended and manipulated in every way possible.

The entrance hall basks in a soft golden light that reflects floor-to-ceiling panels of solar bronze mirror, casting a golden glow on the aubergine carpet used throughout the apartment. A nineteenth-century kilim rug provides a vivid note, and contrasts with the primitive carving of an antique Greek chest. Texture and color are of primary importance to Mr. Dwork. He is attached to the primitive in both art and fabric, strongly believing in the ultimate sophistication of handwork. And contrasting textures allow him the same manipulation of space that the use of color provides.

For example, the sand-colored walls of Madagascar cloth in the living room/study form the ideal background for the owner's collection of primitive art. The designer treats art almost as if he were a museum curator, and he makes an effort to display each piece to its best advantage. But he makes sure that no one piece of art is allowed to dominate the room; each contributes in its own way to the totality of the design.

All upholstered furniture was specifically designed to enhance the works of art in an appropriately sculptural way. The furnishings, in fact, are underplayed, unless they are sufficiently unique and exciting in themselves. This reflects the designer's point of view that furniture is for comfort, not for show. However, he has seen fit to emphasize the architectural detailing of the room by painting it

white in order to frame the many things that serve to make the apartment personal.

The arrangement makes for a good deal of flexibility. A large painting by Barbara Sandler over the fireplace, for example, was added after the interiors were completed. But Mr. Dwork, aware of the needs of collectors and their ever-changing collections, had provided for such contingencies, and the painting is now completely at home. The designer himself is a collector, with a keen interest in art and an enthusiasm for galleries. At one time he collected French faïence and English ceramics, which have since been banished to a closet.

"I don't consider them less good," he says. "It's simply that my tastes have changed, and I've moved in a more contemporary direction. I think the same thing is true of the owner of this apartment."

In line with his belief that convenience and comfort should be the keynotes of good design, Mr. Dwork has given the aubergine bedroom more than one function. Since there is no dining room in the apartment, there is a clearly allotted space in each room for casual meals. In the bedroom, banquettes near the fireplace serve this function, and a pervading atmosphere of informality, quite unlike that of the owner's country house, is created. In this room, as in the others, recessed lighting is used extensively for the creation of mood and definition.

The apartment, then, is thoroughly representative of Melvin Dwork's design techniques and point of view. During the course of his career he has always concentrated on home décor, and he has rarely been involved in commercial projects. "My work," he says, explaining his emphasis, "has always been personalized for the individual."

It is his role, he feels, to influence the people he works for in the most indirect way possible. His function is not to change their personalities or their ways of life; rather, it is to harmonize everything and create a mood of relaxation and confidence. He is not a casual designer, and he believes that everything must have a specific place. Thus, the effect he creates is clean and simple and underplayed. Yet there is a certain evident magic at work, a magic that seems to say, "This is personal."

Designer Melvin Dwork's architectural
orientation influenced the structural changes and
spatial decisions he made for this small
Manhattan apartment. The interplay of light and
dark areas makes rooms seem larger. BELOW: A
kilim rug from Afghanistan seems to vibrate
on the aubergine carpeting of the Entrance Hall.
The linen-mâché sculpture is by Carol Anthony.

In the Living Room, the textured walls, covered with natural woven raffia from Madagascar, and the intentionally underplayed custom furnishings complement an extensive collection of primitive art. Of special note is the African group, including two Dogon carved-wood grainery doors and a helmet, a Luena mask from Angola, and a Mende mask with fiber beard. Contemporary art works, such as the Barbara Sandler painting of an Indian above the fireplace, contrast strikingly with the primitive objects.

103

The dark lacquered walls of the large Bedroom
evoke the feeling of a primeval den. Abundant with
primitive objects, the versatile space also
functions as a sitting room, library and dining
area. LEFT: Geometrically patterned tent trappings
outline sections of the walls and frame a New
Guinea mask painting. The powerful visage of
Ironcloud by Barbara Sandler hangs above the
fireplace; mounted on the wall at right is a Masai
shield. Carpeting extends over the built-in
platforms of banquette and bed; the suede cloth
cushions and bedspread are accented by Indonesian
cotton-covered pillows. Additional seating is
upholstered in contemporary chevron-patterned wool
fabric. ABOVE: Another view reveals
contemporary sculptures: a figure by Carol Anthony
and a fanciful airship by Clifford Earl.

# A RANCH WITH TRADITIONAL GRACE

For the last hundred years, the grand design of the European past has inspired many elegant interiors on the eastern seaboard of the United States. But in the West, where the concept of the small palace seemed incompatible with the wide open spaces, a purely regional style—and a purely American one—had the opportunity to develop.

In a desire to integrate the differing design thrusts of Europe and America, Mr. and Mrs. Deane Johnson of Los Angeles asked the decorating firm of Brown-Buckley to create interiors for their newly acquired Colorado ranch. Designers Logan Brown and Tom Buckley were more than flexible in their approach, and their concepts moved from Versailles to Southampton to Colorado on a tangential curve that results in a stunning synthesis of East and West.

All the ingredients were right, from the beginning. Mr. Johnson himself had a lifelong dream of owning a working cattle ranch. Born and brought up in mother lode country, he spent the early summers of his life riding through gold mining country on a quarter horse, and he retains all his youthful enthusiasm for the western way of life.

On the other hand, his wife, Anne Ford Johnson, is more rooted in eastern traditions, having lived in New York City and Detroit and Long Island. She had long collected antiques of museum quality and had lived a rather more formal life. When she and Mr. Johnson were first married, they made their first home in Los Angeles. Though it had all the informality and openness of the West, it did at the same time suggest the sophistication of an elegant Parisian salon. In some ways this contradictory mixture did not seem entirely satisfactory to the Johnsons. With the acquisition of a ranch house in Colorado, however, they seemed to have resolved the dilemma by putting down their roots more firmly and positively in the western tradition.

Interior designer Tom Buckley, formerly associated with the firm of McMillen, Inc., in New York City, has worked on five of Mrs. Johnson's houses over the course of the last twenty years. In 1969 he formed a partnership with Logan Brown, a graduate of the University of Virginia, where he studied architecture and the fine arts. The partnership is a smooth one and offers two contrasting personalities: Mr. Buckley, urbane and intense, and Mr. Brown, humorous and relaxed. And, unlike many such design partnerships, this one seems to thrive on a star system. The stars, it must be said, do alternate depending on the circumstances.

Having known Mr. Johnson for two decades, Tom Buckley quite naturally took the lead in the Colorado project, and Logan Brown played a secondary role. Often, of course, the reverse is true, and each is flexible enough to do what a given situation calls for. So all the elements were quite in order for beginning the creation of the Johnson ranch in Colorado: designers comfortably familiar with the tastes and way of life of the owners, and owners anxious to cooperate in every way possible. The design of the ranch soon became an intriguing challenge for all concerned.

The setting alone is marvelously natural and dramatic; the ranch itself, remote and private. The approach leads through green fields and over a roaring trout-filled stream. A sudden bend in the road reveals the ranch, with high snow-covered mountains looming in the background. There is more than a hint of the power and majesty of the American wilderness.

At the heart of the 7,500-acre ranch is a compound of three separate buildings: a main house, still to be expanded; a ranger station, built originally in the 1860s; and a rather small two-story guest house, the architecture designed by Deane Johnson himself. The fact that the guest house—with its two large bed/sitting rooms, two baths and kitchen—was the first interior work completed, is characteristic of Anne Johnson's concern as a hostess. It was important to her that the guest house be available as rapidly as possible for her children, for friends from all over the world and for neighboring ranchers. The interiors now bear the signature of her personality, and concern for the comfort of her guests is everywhere apparent. On the bedside tables are carafes of ice water, bowls of fruit, and books. Vases are filled with fresh flowers.

However attractive the guest house may be, it is in the main house that the full impact of Mrs.

Johnson's personality, so well interpreted by designers Buckley and Brown, can be felt.

"If I were building a house today in Long Island," she says, "I really think I would want the interiors to look like the ones here in the ranch house. My tastes have changed a good deal."

It is true that many of the furnishings and accessories in the main house have come from her former residences, but the difference in arrangement and décor is striking and the overall effect is, of course, totally different.

"Twenty years ago in the East, her upholstered pieces would have been covered in silk velvet," Logan Brown comments. "Today they're covered in cotton tweed. Rugs would have been Aubusson; but now at the ranch they are Portuguese needlepoint. Wallcoverings are cotton, rather than silk damask, and French silk lamp shades have given way to painted paper shades. There is no longer the desire to have Louis XVI fabrics on Louis XVI chairs. The museum look is gone, and period chairs here at the ranch are covered in checked cotton. The furniture is still exquisite, needless to say, but it has been made casual and livable."

Easy maintenance is the keynote of the ranch, and the staff required is minimal. Mr. Johnson and his foreman watch over the herds of Hereford and Black Angus cattle, and Mrs. Johnson supervises the inside of the ranch house.

In fact, a good deal of the entertaining takes place in the kitchen itself, and guests are often given specific chores to do. Activity centers around a large chopping block hung with heavy French pots and pans. Dinners are served informally on a table covered with a Peruvian quilt; the tableware is Country French; the flatware, stainless steel. Everything is done very simply, but the wines are the finest and the butter is rolled.

"I'm trying to simplify my life," reflects Mrs. Johnson thoughtfully. "People don't live the way they once did, and I'm not really sure they want to anymore. I know that I don't want the responsibility of a great many possessions now. And I would rather have this ranch than any amount of great paintings or antique porcelains."

ABOVE: *The road approaching the ranch of Mr. and Mrs. Deane Johnson in the Colorado mountains passes through green fields where peacefully grazing horses are enclosed by white fences.* OPPOSITE: *The compound, with its main house, ranger station and two-story guest-house, lies amid the green belt that faces the mountain cliffs; it comprises the heart of a working cattle ranch.* LEFT: *Designers Logan Brown and Tom Buckley created a rustic effect in this Hallway. The warm-toned paisley wallcovering and random-cut native fir floors are both simple and suitable. Mrs. Johnson has arranged local wild flowers and grasses around a 17th-century English table.*

109

BELOW: *A fireplace of native moss rock, a mantel shelf rescued from a derelict barn, flowered chintz wall and furniture coverings and lively plaid carpeting instill a country atmosphere in the Living Room of the main house.* LOWER: *Arrayed on a massive butcher-block table in the Living Room is a collection of small antiques, including an English miner's lunch pail.*

BELOW: *A Guest Room is enlivened by a collection of 18th-century French engravings and by rugs cut from a single 19th-century French needlepoint carpet. The redwood walls are painted and frosted in cool shades that reflect the verdant landscape.* LOWER: *The feeling is informal in the Kitchen/Dining Room of the main house, where the table is draped with a Peruvian quilt.*

ABOVE: *Soft curtains, with cord pulls and old-fashioned smocked headings, frame the windows in an alcove of the Double Guest Room.* RIGHT: *Beyond the small 19th-century Dutch wire and wood-ball chandelier is a view of the mid-19th-century ranger station, other ranch buildings and the majestic mountains.* OPPOSITE: *The Blue Guest Room recalls European country hospitality. Rough plaster walls are crossed with red fir beams. The carved bed with horse-hoof feet has an open, ruffled canopy. Other furnishings include a 17th-century Italian writing table, a Louis XV bedside table, Delft lamps and Tibetan rugs adorned with dragon and phoenix motifs.*

# THE LIBERATION
# OF COMPACT
# DIMENSIONS

The design is sophisticated, formal, contemporary—in its own way a graphic definition of style. The context could be Paris or Milan or New York. That the interiors are in Beverly Hills, California, simply indicates a universality of design language. Dramatic and personal, the result is nevertheless restrained and carefully controlled.

It started years ago at the shop of an antiques dealer in New York City. There Sally Sirkin Lewis, now a Los Angeles interior designer and showroom owner, first saw the Japanese screen that so influences the design theme of her new house.

"For a long time the screen had been folded up in the back of the shop," she remembers, "and I had been asking to see it regularly."

Finally the dealer opened the screen for her, revealing an intriguing scene of Oriental cranes. The image stayed indelibly with the designer and now, years later, a similar flock of birds swoops silently around the walls of the Lewis home in Beverly Hills. Painted directly on soft gold-leafed paper, the birds—translated into actuality by Arthur Fine from the designer's description—circle endlessly through the living room and dining room.

The effect is riveting, and the painted cranes instantly command the attention of anyone entering the house. Against a background of ebony floors, and banquettes covered in white Indian cotton, this dramatic echo of an antique Japanese screen is more than simply a keynote of the interior design; it makes as strong a statement about the interior designer herself—about Sally Sirkin Lewis and her determination. "I have always wanted to let my fancy fly," she says, "to do something terribly innovative and imaginative.

"As a professional designer," she adds, "I nearly always have to suppress these wishes. Many people would think of them as outlandish, or simply examples of pure fantasy. But this design was my own, for my husband and myself, and I was able to do something I didn't have to explain to anybody. Incidentally, that's a marvelous feeling for an interior designer!"

Her original plans for the new house had been rather different: "Very Milan, brushed steel walls,

114

brass moldings, geometric carpets, lots of velour." The more she thought about the projected design, however, the more unoriginal she found it to be. It had all been done before. She decided to indulge her flair for the dramatic, instead, and the vision of an antique Japanese screen covered with exotic birds surfaced in her mind. She decided to give free rein to her active imagination.

"Everything happened the night I came to that decision," she says. "The whole house was designed in my mind—the banquettes, the colors, the sisal matting, the blinds, the dining room pieces. Everything happened that night. I put it all down on paper, and it was exactly what I wanted."

This was not the first time the designer had changed her mind about the new house. In fact, when she and her husband first decided to move from a larger Beverly Hills home—their children being grown—she had fixed ideas about what form the new house should take.

"Don't bother to show me a house with less than ten-foot ceilings," she told the real estate brokers. "And don't show me a house that doesn't have separate rooms—separate living room, separate dining room, separate everything. Don't show me anything with sliding doors."

Inevitably, the house she and her husband finally bought had every one of the elements she had indicated she disliked—even eight-foot ceilings, which she particularly hates.

"I can't explain it," says Mrs. Lewis. "Even with all these defects—at least they were defects to me— the house had a marvelously appealing atmosphere. I can't describe it exactly, but it was something I hadn't seen anyplace else."

The house, with one bedroom and a study that doubles as a guest room, is small. A certain number of structural changes had to be made, and the designer turned windows into glass doors that open to a deck she added. The garden that lies between the house and the wall shielding it from the street now has an Oriental feeling, quite in keeping with the mood of the interiors.

The entrance hall itself gives an immediate cue to the drama within, with its walls lined in black glass. It is a drama that played for so long in the designer's imagination that, for her, there are no surprises left. Even when it was first completed, the room did not shock her.

"As a matter of fact, my clients are always surprised that I'm so calm when installation is taking place," says Mrs. Lewis. "But you see, I know exactly what everything is going to look like. Exactly. There were no disappointments for me in this house, nothing that I would have done differently.

"But there was one amusing moment during the installation. I had just come in as they started to put the gold-leafed paper down on the walls. It was about noon on a very sunny day, and I thought to myself, 'We're all going to go blind!' But of course that was before the birds were painted on the wall. That project took the better part of four months, and there were carpenters and electricians and moving men all over the place."

"It was really quite calm," says Arthur Fine, the artist. "I simply moved from wall to wall, as the other work was going on. Sally stood there with incredible poise, directing the whole operation like a symphony conductor."

The work was finished, the house is complete and the designer herself looks very much at home. Her honey-colored hair blends with the soft gold of the walls creating an image of harmony.

"I guess the interiors do express me," she says. "I've always worn white and brown and beige."

The pillows heaped on the white banquettes; the black mantel; the browns and beiges of bedroom and sitting room—all provide a fitting background for her. The house is right, too, for the kind of entertaining she and her husband enjoy.

"I only entertain the people I truly enjoy being with," she says. "We don't give large parties. But I do like to have people over often—two or four or six. The living room happens to be marvelously arranged for the way we entertain. We'll have dinner, and then we'll sit on the banquettes and talk until two o'clock in the morning. It's just my kind of house. It really is. The style is right for me."

And so it is. And style is definitely what Sally Sirkin Lewis is all about.

Cranes in flight, inspired by a Japanese painted screen of the Muromachi Period, seem to soar across the gold-leafed tea-papered Living Room walls in the Beverly Hills home of designer Sally Sirkin Lewis. Rough-surfaced black rock tables and sisal matting reinforce the natural feeling, while the Oriental flavor is enhanced by a black-lacquered mantel and a Japanese tea table.

The Arthur Fine mural extends
into an intimate Dining Area
where antique Japanese lacquered
trays, poised upon a buffet of
faux-porphyry lacquer, echo the
bird motif. Stately Japanese
lacquered candlesticks illuminate a
glass-topped table. Like an inky
pool, the surface of the table reflects
the mural image of birds in
flight. The note of lightness
introduced by pale candles and
white-bodied painted birds is
expanded by the hand-loomed
Indian cotton that covers the
Chippendale-style chairs.

A Chinese stone fish presides regally in the combination Study/Guest Room. Walls covered with black-lacquered paper and a floor of ebony wood dramatically offset the soft lines and light tones of a sofa bed and slipper chairs. In sharp contrast are a boldly patterned zebra-skin rug and bright raw silk pillows. The low table covered in Madagascar linen adds another natural texture.

*A Los Angeles nightscape provides a glistening background for Terrace dining. White duck is used consistently for the awning, chair cushions and tablecloth. The natural theme, evident throughout the house, here determines even such small details as the seashell napkin rings and bamboo-handled flatware. Chairs that retain an outer layer of bark provide strong textural interest.*

A Japanese bronze Buddha and a totemic wooden sculpture from Africa represent self-contained presences inhabiting the Master Bedroom/Sitting Room. A boldly patterned geometric carpet unifies the room. The varied textures of Indian cotton, silk and velvet are distributed among upholstery, bed canopy and cushions, while a Lucite sculpture stand and low table remain practically invisible. Brass consoles, a brass wall disc and gold-leafed containers radiate light and sheen as they contribute to the sensuous atmosphere.

# ART

# COLLECTOR'S

# RESIDENCE

Give a designer proper architecture, good antiques and great paintings as elements to work with, interior designer Mark Hampton believes, and the decoration almost looks after itself.

"Design is much more than a combination of fabulous fabrics and furniture and an expensive apartment," he explains. "It has to do with the possessions and personality of the owner."

For the present project Mr. Hampton had ample opportunity to prove the efficacy of his theory, since the owner of the apartment is a personal friend as well as being an enthusiastic collector. He offered the designer a choice of everything from Renaissance bronzes and Matisse drawings to contemporary paintings of note.

Although Mr. Hampton insists that an expensive apartment is not at all a necessary condition for good interior decoration, this eighteen-room duplex on Manhattan's Upper East Side did not exactly prove a hindrance. The dramatic setting—with a view of the East River on one side and the panoramic sweep of the city on the other—provides a splendid backdrop for the owner's ever-growing collection of art and antiques.

The focal point of the apartment is a large, rectangular downstairs living room. Completely changed from the traditional furniture-filled room to a stark, gallerylike space, it forms the display case for an extensive collection of contemporary art. A large Kenneth Noland dominates a wall, and four primary-colored Ellsworth Kelly panels hang at one end of the room over a specially designed banquette. A Morris Louis canvas covers a good portion of another wall, and there is a black-and-white Barnett Newman composition over the fireplace. To soften the museumlike mood of the room, the floor has been redone in a combination of bleached and natural oak parquet in a striking geometric pattern.

"It was our intention to have a 'young' atmosphere in all the rooms we worked on," says Mr. Hampton. "Many of the furnishings are traditional, of course, but we felt they would have a fresher look in a contemporary setting."

The result is an eclectic mix filled with delightful counterpoints—bright, youthful and sophisticated. Louis XVI chairs take on new life, covered in café-au-lait suede. A dark lacquered Chinese table, holding a pair of marble Roman busts, a Korean deer and an Oriental head, stands in contrast to the swirling colors of the Noland painting above.

Mark Hampton's point of view is that a man's castle must have many aspects, whether his home happens to be a retreat in the country or a penthouse in New York City.

"In every dwelling," he insists, "there must be formal rooms and informal ones; a place for receptions to be held as well as a place for reading and for watching television."

He has followed this concept to the letter, and the five rooms he has redesigned in the duplex project moods as multifaceted as the interests of the owner himself. Near the living room, for example, a mirrored entrance hall is adorned with a small Henry Moore drawing and a Rococo English Regency cabinet made of velvet and bamboo and leather studded with nails. The gallery, one of the most individual rooms of all, is situated at the end of the entrance hall. With a terra-cotta tile floor, lacquered walls and green plants, it strongly suggests another time and another place—echoing the collector's many travels in search of new and fascinating acquisitions. The room was conceived as a showcase for European and American drawings, among them works by Delacroix and Burne-Jones. The walls are crowded, but it is the intentional clutter of the serious collector.

Other parts of the room reflect the same catholic approach to design. Counterpoints abound: Art Nouveau chairs covered in green velvet; a large nineteenth-century Italian table; photographs of family and friends in silver frames; an English Gothic Revival chair; a cabinet containing a collection of antique glass bells. The only structural change Mark Hampton made in the gallery was the installation of sliding glass doors to replace the original French doors leading to the terrace.

A small foyer and a winding staircase provide additional settings for works of art. A geometric Franz Kline covers one wall, and a George Segal plaster sculpture nestles in the curve of the stairway.

There are innumerable fine drawings by modern masters like Henri Matisse, Egon Schiele, Alberto Giacometti and Alexander Calder.

Upstairs the small drawing room is designed for comfort and relaxation—for going about with bare feet and blue jeans, for smoking a favorite pipe or stretching out with a good book.

"It's one of the most informal rooms in the apartment," says the designer. "But it does serve a particular function as a setting for the owner's collection of architectural drawings."

The room itself is warm and inviting. The colors are rich and soft: dark brown lacquered walls, a brown and beige carpet patterned in a geometric needlepoint. In deliberate contrast to the rest of the apartment, Mr. Hampton chose a floral chintz for the long curtains and comfortable sofas and chairs. The walls are hung with old drawings in antique frames, and a bright green parrot prattles in a corner cage. The effect is charming, if a trifle unnerving.

But the white serenity of Mark Hampton's overall theme reappears once more in the master bedroom. Large and cool, its white lacquered walls glisten like the sun on water. The bed itself is white, covered in geometrically stitched linen matched by the curtains at the long windows. The mood is furthered by the bleached cabinet hanging over the fireplace and the bleached floor spread with an antique Tibetan rug, gently faded by age.

Quite naturally this room, like the others, is the setting for further collections: tiny objects fill a mother-of-pearl cabinet, a group of small boxes shaped like shoes march along a bedside table that hides a sophisticated stereo system, and Indian and Persian miniatures adorn the walls.

The apartment, basically a repository for an enthusiastic collector's accumulation of treasures, might well have been as expressionless as a museum vault. Instead it projects an aura of comfort, individuality and practicality. Mark Hampton takes only a modest amount of credit.

"The success or failure of an apartment like this depends to a large extent on the taste and understanding of the owner," he says. "I was extremely fortunate in that respect."

The 32-by-20-foot Living Room of an 18-room
Manhattan duplex was conceived by designer
Mark Hampton as a showcase for a growing
collection of modern art and antiquities. Four
panels by Ellsworth Kelly, a Kenneth Noland
target painting and a custom-designed oak
parquetry floor establish a geometric context.
Antique appointments create a counterpoint.

*The mirrored Entrance Hall infinitely reflects an unusual lacquered and studded Regency cabinet of velvet, bamboo and leather; two French retour d'Egypte bronze heads above it echo the deep rich tones and gilt ornamentation. The drawing of a nude by British sculptor Henry Moore introduces a 20th-century note and causes a blending of the antique and the contemporary.*

RIGHT: *Opening onto a terrace with a splendid panoramic vista of Manhattan, the Gallery houses favorite photographs, drawings and, in a massive 18th-century English breakfront, a cache of delicate glass bells. A 19th-century Italian table and low French stools mix effortlessly with a sinuous Art Nouveau velvet-upholstered armchair.*
BELOW: *Comfort is a primary consideration in the small upstairs Drawing Room, which features a collection of 19th-century objects and memorabilia in an Edwardian atmosphere. Dark lacquered walls provide a dramatic backdrop for tiers of primarily 17th- and 18th-century architectural drawings by Italian artists.*

126

LEFT: *Curving around the winding staircase is a wall lined with drawings, including those by Lachaise, Matisse, Schiele, Klimpt, Calder, Lindner, Hockney and Giacometti.* BELOW: *The Master Bedroom, which enjoys a view of the East River, glistens with white lacquered walls and a stainless-steel fireplace and bedframe. An English whatnot cabinet and an ebony and mother-of-pearl vitrine display an assortment of ivory objects, while the walls are adorned with an intriguing collection of Persian and Indian miniatures.*

# CALIFORNIA PENTHOUSE— A NEW VIEW

One of the great contemporary myths and a compelling image of sophisticated living has always been the New York penthouse apartment. In the popular imagination it is a luxurious dwelling filled with glamorous and influential people, poised dramatically over Central Park.

Oddly enough, it is rapidly becoming a symbol of California, as well. Indeed, like so much else, the concept of the penthouse apartment—the concept of high-rise living in general—has been carried across the Great Plains to the Pacific Coast, undergoing a sea change in the process—and a rather happy one.

During the first half of the twentieth century there was little reason for tall buildings in southern California, and the San Andreas Fault seemed to preclude them. But new technology, the pressures of population and the transformation of Los Angeles— to take one city—into a crowded metropolis created the need for vertical space. Naturally this process has occurred in every part of the United States, but it has been more rapid and often more exaggerated in southern California. It is surprising that more Californians have not resisted the vertical thrust so alien to their surroundings. And now in Los Angeles there are many interior designers who have embraced the concept of high-rise living with enthusiasm and are hurrying to meet the future.

Frank Austin is one such enthusiast. As a designer, his reasons for having committed himself to apartment living are at once practical and aesthetic. There is nothing unusual about his commitment except—and the exception is important—that it has taken place in the context of southern California. It is, of course, an area that has attracted people because of climate and scenery and the chance to enjoy comfort and privacy near green lawns and palm trees, beaches and swimming pools. What possible advantage could there be in having an apartment in a spacious city like Los Angeles?

With characteristic firmness Frank Austin indicates that there are many—so many, in fact, that they far outweigh the possible disadvantages. He is a New Yorker by origin, it is true, but this circumstance influences his point of view very little. His own penthouse looks down from the top of a high rise, and the morning view on a clear day stretches all the way to the Pacific Ocean and takes in an area from Palos Verdes to Malibu. It is a view, he points out, that even the most bemused New Yorker must regard with a certain amount of awe. In the evening the city lights sparkling below him in every direction are impressive. But the view is Mr. Austin's least important reason for being enthusiastic about what is, in his own fortunate case, penthouse living. Function and practicality are the real reasons.

It may be surprising to find such determined practicality in a designer with extravagant tastes and expansive ideas. Tall and energetic, with the confidence of innumerable jobs well done, Frank Austin indicates, and his manner leaves no room for doubt, that apartment living has come to California for good. And about time, too, in his view. He feels it is far less expensive to own or rent an apartment than to worry about the maintenance of a private house—particularly, as he observes, "in these uncertain times." There is also the matter of convenience. He can, of course, turn the key and leave for long periods—as he frequently does, on buying trips to Europe and South America—without having to worry about maintenance or concern himself with the gardener, the pool man or any other member of the household staff. More important, he feels, is the fact that as an interior designer he has found in the basic simplicity—indeed, in the lack of character—of the apartment blueprint the ideal background for his own compositions. Far more flexibility of design is possible without the restrictions that a house of a particular period might impose.

His penthouse apartment is a good illustration of this point: actually it is two apartments in one, a 4,000-square-foot area made to appear even larger through the skillful use of mirrors, windows and lighting. Because of Frank Austin's insistence, the lighting is based "on the eighteenth-century candle." Candelabras dominate while auxiliary lighting systems are underplayed. This professional concern with detail is also evident in the apartment's most notable feature: its space and easy flow. Furniture is exquisite and elaborately detailed—a composite of unusual antiques—all the more reason to have a

simple background. Mr. Austin insists upon quality in everything: down pillows and the finest fabrics, for instance. But patterns are of the simplest. Everything is arranged for comfort and flexibility, and two people can be entertained as pleasantly and effectively as two hundred.

The décor can be changed at will, without the necessity for any architectural change. This amount of freedom would surely not be possible within the context of a typical Georgian or Tudor house, for example, where architecture itself might well dictate the direction of interior décor.

So there are important advantages from the design point of view in apartment living, and Frank Austin is more than happy to discuss them. The resulting decoration in his own penthouse is dramatic; even, to some tastes, flamboyant. But Mr. Austin is not a retiring person. If you are going to do a proper job, Mr. Austin suggests, you might as well allow yourself to go all the way.

His own approach has relied to a large extent on the traditional, but he feels that the spare and functional design of the contemporary apartment provides for any number of different interpretations. It can, and should, embrace and overcome the challenges of contemporary living.

To Mr. Austin's mind, flexibility of approach is the great advantage of apartment living. He can, of course, design the interiors of banks and houses and nightclubs—he has done them all—but his preference now is for apartment décor.

"Today it is more important than ever," he says, "to understand the concept of apartment living. It is essential for the interior designer, particularly now, particularly here in southern California. It represents the direction of the future, I think, and we, as designers, must accept that fact and deal with it."

He has not imposed an alien style on Los Angeles. But as a New Yorker he has long understood the nature of apartment living and its many advantages. Like so many other Californians, he is now enjoying a way of life borrowed from less hospitable climates and subtly changed to reflect the freedom and the sun and the many varieties of an appealing new dispensation.

LEFT: *A subtle fusion of color values and textures characterizes the Living Room of designer Frank Austin's 4,000-square-foot Los Angeles penthouse apartment. Stylized landscape elements embellish a late-17th-century twelve-panel coromandel screen, which blends with the warm-toned velvet wall and sofa upholstery, a suede-covered English ladder-back chair and the parquet flooring.*

ABOVE: *A pair of 18th-century French chinoiserie carved figures with animated gestures and an antique Venetian mirror face the Living Room. An Italian Louis XVI gilt chair and an elaborately ornamented Korean tortoiseshell and lacquer chest add to the rich mix.*

131

OPPOSITE: *Another view of the Living Room points up its free-flowing spaciousness, gently illuminated by an 18th-century candelabrum, soft overhead lighting and the glowing lights of the city. Grouped near the large sliding glass doors are a Regency pedestal table and four Louis XV cane-backed chairs. In front of the piano is an Empire parcel gilt chair with figural hocked legs.*

ABOVE: *A silver-plated Art Nouveau chandelier hangs above the Dining Room's Régence cane-backed armchairs and English Sheraton mahogany table. Many tall tapers in both crystal and bronze candelabras illustrate Mr. Austin's desire to base the lighting "on the 18th-century candle." Other furnishings include an 18th-century George II gilt pier mirror and an 18th-century French bombé console holding a Derby tureen.*

An English four-poster bed with paneled canopy
and headboard, used by the Duke of Windsor in
his youth, dominates the Master Bedroom. Two
18th-century American primitive portraits and an
American Federalist gilt eagle are mounted on
the grass cloth wallcovering. The boldly patterned
carpet strikes a note of contemporary contrast
and echoes the living room parquet.

*A natural advantage of penthouse living is the exhilarating view from the Terrace. At night the lights of the city sparkle and by day the panorama stretches all the way to the Pacific, taking in an area that extends from the Palos Verdes Peninsula to Malibu. A contemporary tablesetting of pottery and glass contrasts with the weblike Victorian painted wire dining table and chairs.*

# NEW
# DESIGN
# IN THE
# OLD
# DAKOTA

The Dakota—that magnificent Gothic apartment house in Manhattan, the city's first—has always been a challenge for interior designers. In Thomas Britt's case the challenge was heightened by the rather laconic instructions of the international businessman who engaged him: "Give me a place where I can live and work quietly, and entertain well, too."

More restrained than other Britt interiors—the designer's highly personalized style frequently leans to the dramatic—the result is a contemporary solution that combines a versatile use of space with furnishings of considerable splendor.

The designer himself feels naturally drawn to "simple luxury," "beautiful quality" and "glorious antiques." He is interested in anything from pre-Columbian art to Orientalia.

"I call what I do *decorating*," says Mr. Britt. "But I believe it really is *design*. This is particularly true in the present design. The challenge was an interesting one for me, since no two apartments in The Dakota are alike. This apartment naturally had the famous high ceilings and the splendid architectural detailing, but it did consist of a number of small rooms. But the building is really the only one in the city that has the true look and feel of a Parisian apartment house. I wanted to retain all that romanticism, and at the same time evoke the feeling of today."

He has managed to accomplish the updating with panache, and it is a refreshing surprise to come out of the Victorian somberness of one of The Dakota's hallways into the sleek new Britt design.

"It's a very masculine apartment, developed around a theme of almost no color," says the designer. "It's mostly black, *tête-de-nègre* or rich shades of brown. The only really vibrant color in the apartment comes from paintings by Poliakoff, Ossorio and others.

"But color did not really present much of a problem. The real problems came about, I think, because of the architecture of the space itself. The front living room, for example, had no wall space to speak of. There were doors everyplace and only one window, and just two wall areas were the same. In order to give the room some coherent shape I designed *L*-shaped banquettes to flank the fireplace.

I do think it's wrong to disguise things if a room doesn't have strong architectural qualities of its own. So I concentrate on furniture arrangement."

The designer has followed this point of view with consistency throughout the apartment. The squarish living room, walls covered in Belgian linen, contains a custom-designed sofa and several banquettes. The sofa seems to float in the middle of the room, loosely anchored by a black-lacquered table and a large ottoman. The fact is that such a grouping of furniture has become almost a Britt trademark.

Because there are few lamps in the apartment, the designer has made extensive use of track lights and recessed spots. "I felt the need for special lighting," he explains, "largely because most of the artwork demanded it. As a matter of fact, this was the first time I'd ever worked with a double-circuit track, and I'm enchanted with the variety of effects it has on interior space."

Next to the living room is a library, with a velvet banquette, more paintings, many books and records and an amber glass desk on a bronze base, another Thomas Britt design.

"This is the room where the owner works during the day," says the designer. "And at night he has guests in for cocktails and conversation and after-dinner coffee. It's also the music room. That seems to cover a lot of ground, but I do see a tremendous need today for each room to serve many purposes. In fact, I designed the entire apartment around that premise."

Indeed he has, and his work at The Dakota provides a number of possible solutions to some of the limitations of contemporary living. Most people, even those with the means, no longer have those generous houses and apartments of the past, with a room for every pleasure and every necessity. Gone now are the ballrooms, the billiard rooms, the flower rooms, the sewing rooms, the silver rooms. Today's scale of living is considerably reduced, and versatility of space must be considered as never before.

Throughout the course of the design Mr. Britt never lost sight of his original goal: the creation of multipurpose rooms. The dining room is an excellent example. Reached through a narrow hallway lined with Rouault lithographs, its focus is a sensuously curved banquette. There is a glass dining room table, similar to the one in the library, several seventeenth-century Japanese vases and a half dozen Louise Nevelson drawings on the wall. All of the art and furniture seem to extend the limits of a small room in every direction.

"The owner lives here alone most of the time," says Mr. Britt. "But his children do come to visit several times a year for long periods. Then, if he wishes, he can use the dining room as another living room. The kind of functional arrangement I've provided allows him the luxury of choice."

That luxury has been provided throughout the apartment. The master bedroom, for example, is a room of ordinary size, but a large bed with double rows of pillows has given it an extra dimension and the character of a sitting room.

"Enormous scale is what I was after," says the designer. "It gives the space the drama necessary for the atmosphere The Dakota itself provides. And you know, it is a delight to be able to work with the unusual and old-fashioned space of a building like this. The average person might not think so, but it is ideal as a background for contemporary décor."

The dramatic interplay between traditional architecture and contemporary décor is a provocative one, and one that the designer has utilized to great advantage. This sort of interplay is not often possible in the context of the usual modern apartment—more often than not, a series of cold and sterile cubes. Perhaps that is why some European decoration seems far more effective than its counterpart in the United States, for in Europe the interior designer is very likely to have the opportunity of making a contemporary statement against the softer backdrop of traditional architectural design and detailing. Such is one of the great advantages of working with the space of The Dakota, for example.

Using the materials at hand and his own contemporary talents, Mr. Britt has created an apartment for all purposes and all seasons. "I don't like a lot of overcrowding," he says. "And I appreciate a neat and clean kind of drama. I really think I'm engaged in editing, as much as in designing."

Thomas Britt's innovative design for an apartment in New York's legendary Gothic apartment house The Dakota involved a total transformation of the existing space. He gave each of the small, high-ceilinged rooms a dramatically larger sense of scale. OPPOSITE: A colorful Poliakoff painting and a primitive African mask complement the contemporary look of the Entrance Hall, with its shiny vinyl-covered walls and dark-stained floors. ABOVE LEFT: A vibrant Ossorio painting adds color accents to the Living Room. Overhead track lighting and pale strié linen-wrapped walls enhance the art. CENTER LEFT: L-shaped banquettes and two Poliakoff paintings flank the Living Room fireplace, a detail characteristic of The Dakota's impressive architecture. A Japanese vase and a Trova sculpture stand on the black-lacquered table behind the sofa. BELOW LEFT: Through a wide doorway, a painting by the Spanish artist Tapies seems to glow against the dark vinyl-covered walls of the Library adjacent to the living room; beneath the canvas is a plush banquette.

*Stark contrast predominates in the Guest Room, which is occupied several months each year by the owner's children. Bolstered twin beds and leather-covered Barcelona chairs merge with the floor and the walls, while moldings and vertical blinds, bookshelves and desk add a crisp linear quality. Small reading lamps are at hand.*

Although narrow, the space of the Master Bedroom is expanded by the built-in nature of the design and the unifying quality of a rich corduroy fabric used for the draperies and bedcovering. Doris Caesar's sculpture Kneeling Woman sits on one of the two custom-designed laminated plastic boxes that serve as bedside tables and conveniently house electrical switches.

# A FILMMAKER'S TOWNHOUSE

In Beverly Hills, not far from Sunset Boulevard, are a pair of iron gates and a modest brick wall. Behind this unassuming exterior, however, lies a miniature domain, passably regal even for Beverly Hills: two acres of green lawns and towering trees along a winding driveway lined with statues. It is a place of fountains and rose bushes, of peace and enviable privacy. In the interests of popular mythology, it is fitting that this small kingdom belongs to the head of production at a major motion picture studio.

Robert Evans is that filmmaker—young for the position he holds, young for the skill with which he has supervised the creation of a gracious setting for his personal life. It is a setting he created—"half and half," in his words—with interior designer Robert Benton and with all the drive and search for perfection that mark his own career in films. Mr. Evans may be young, but his ideas about the house and property are precise and his thoughts about décor are very clearly articulated.

"I'm terribly meticulous," he says. "And I tend to be very decisive. Too much so, I imagine. It can be a detriment, since many times I'm wrong. I must be almost impossible to work with, and Bob Benton deserves all kinds of praise and credit for his endless patience and understanding.

"Perhaps the reason I'm so meticulous and make such an attempt to be a perfectionist—all possible psychological reasons aside—is that I think a house, like a film, is the culmination of a thousand nuances. Success lies in the details."

Situated in the middle of a green fastness that could be in Europe or in any part of the eastern United States, the house itself is surprisingly small. Basically it is a townhouse in the French style, built in 1942 by the California architect John Woolf. One of his earliest works, its design has been imitated often, and its influence has been far-reaching. Today the mansard roof is one of the most popular details of California architecture, and it is in keeping with a growing enthusiasm in the United States for European antiques and, in particular, for French furniture, both formal and informal.

The definition of the Evans residence as a "townhouse" is somewhat misleading. Its estatelike setting forms the basis for the contradiction. The house faces a courtyard, in the middle of which is a fountain, and beyond that a generous lawn, an oval swimming pool and a second building containing the requisite screening room, projection booth and offices of a filmmaker. A tennis court and a small greenhouse complete the amenities, the whole shielded from the outside world by great stands of cypress and eucalyptus—many of them 200 feet tall. At one side of the lawn the enormous gnarled branches of a 400-year-old sycamore overhang an outdoor dining area. In May and June the entire property is rich with bursts of many-colored roses, perhaps five thousand in all.

The interior of the main building, on the other hand, conforms to the townhouse theme. There are not many rooms, nor are they large, but they are sophisticated in an essentially urban manner.

"I wanted a look of my own," says Mr. Evans. "At the beginning I had definite ideas about what form it should take. Many of these ideas changed as we went along, but the general effect remains: dark wood furniture and floors, monochromatic beiges for fabrics and subtle tones of silk velvet on the walls. In any event, Bob Benton and I concentrated on the background first.

"Since it is my profession, I'm inclined to think in film terms about almost everything I do. And I feel very strongly that the background is the most important element in a motion picture. It enriches the foreground—not the other way around, as amateurs are inclined to think. The same thing in décor: furniture and accessories are almost the last matters that should be considered whereas backgrounds are basic and a proper starting point."

The living room itself is the best illustration of that combination of film technique and interior décor Mr. Evans is describing. The room is not large, and two comfortable beige sofas extend toward the fireplace with a long table between them. There are antique statues, fine drawings and paintings, books, magazines, any number of striking accessories. But, as Mr. Evans explains, the foreground is not what he considers to be the important thing. The background is.

The focal point of the room is a graceful Louis XVI mantel, set into a glass wall. Instead of the usual arrangement, the chimney flues rise upward through pilasters at each side of the mantel, and above and around the mantel there is an unobstructed view of the outside. The idea is not new, Mr. Evans explains; it was copied from a similar fireplace treatment at *Malmaison*, the country home of Napoleon and Josephine. However, there is nothing similar in this country.

Perhaps even more unusual than the architectural effect the glass wall provides is a stunning optical illusion arranged by Mr. Evans—an illusion quite in keeping with motion picture technique. At night, and often during the day, a blazing fire is set in the fireplace. Hundreds of feet away, in the screening room, beyond the courtyard and the lawn and the swimming pool, an identical fire has been set and lined up precisely with the one in the living room. The effect is magical, giving the visual impression that the living room fire itself is reflected in the glass wall above it. The owner has followed his own advice exactly: The background has become the most important aspect of the living room.

"Certainly it's a cliché to say that nothing reflects a person more than his own house," Mr. Evans remarks. "I've been in so many elaborate houses—far more elaborate than this one—that have no character at all. Either they were done carte blanche by a decorator, and seemed impersonal, or they were ostentatious. Another cliché: Taste has very little to do with money. Certainly I'm not denying that some things here were expensive. But when I was living in New York City in a modest rented apartment, it had my special look, too."

Happily, he has not had to compromise in his present house, but he is by no means finished with it. There are many plans for the future: a guest house, the redecoration of his bedroom and bath, among other projects. And all of it will take place in the context of two acres of hidden forest, at once convenient to and entirely removed from, the bustle and activity of Beverly Hills and Los Angeles.

"It's really perfect for me," says Mr. Evans. "Since I'm a very private person."

LEFT: *The Living Room of film producer Robert Evans's French-style townhouse in Beverly Hills expresses his desire for a look of meticulous sophistication. The unusual fireplace treatment was copied from Malmaison: a Louis XVI mantel is set into a glass wall, and the chimney flues are diverted behind pilasters flanking the mantel—leaving the overmantel open to an outdoor view.*

ABOVE: *Another Living Room view shows the warm-toned wood elements—doors, moldings and columns, as well as the parquet floor—that create a richly defined atmosphere for a collection that focuses on French modern art. Because Mr. Evans believes that backgrounds are even more important than foregrounds, special consideration was given by designer Robert Benton to the architectural detailing of the residence.*

RIGHT: *A masculine atmosphere prevails in the intimate, paneled room that serves alternatively as the Breakfast, Supper and Card Room. Contributing to the tone are dark Louis XV–style appointments—a table and four high-backed, leather-upholstered chairs—and a series of wall-mounted horse brasses.* OPPOSITE: *A lighter feeling emanates from the Dining Room, which is also furnished in the refined style of Louis XV, with comfortable overscaled armchairs and a large parquetry-topped table. The room is unified by a subtly patterned linen used for draperies, wallcovering, upholstery, and for the lampshades of the carved and painted Italian sconces. A floral composition by contemporary French painter Bernard Buffet adds a bright accent.*

ABOVE: *Separated from the main house by the swimming pool and surrounding flagstone terrace is a structure that includes a large Screening Room, projection booth, kitchen and the dressing rooms that serve poolside guests. The entrance is framed by niches filled with backlit bronze urns. A collection of art posters is highlighted by the large Toulouse-Lautrec above the fireplace.*

OPPOSITE: *Neutral colors promote a sense of restfulness for the Master Bedroom. Two Louis XV benches at the foot of the bed, and a distinctive headboard made from antique French cabinet doors, are upholstered in calfskin. Among the carefully chosen accessories are a polished metal strong box and a pair of carved-wood griffins that have been converted into bedside lamps.*

Beneath the spreading branches of a 400-year-old sycamore tree, one of several outdoor dining areas on Mr. Evans's secluded two-acre estate awaits a luncheon party. A few steps away is the oval swimming pool that intervenes between the main house and the projection house. The vista of tall trees and lush lawns, flowers and potted plants, heightens a sense of total privacy and luxurious ease. When night falls, nature is aided by artifice: The venerable sycamore and all of the surrounding gardens are subtly illuminated in a manner suggestive of moonlight.

# A STATEMENT OF ELEGANT INTROSPECTION

When it comes to dealing with their own environment, many interior designers seem to develop a sense of reticence, even awkwardness. The result is that few such personal statements can be ranked among the most representative work of the creators. This is a curious situation. After all, many designers admit to having become fairly astute psychologists in the course of their careers, having learned to intuit the complex and often contradictory wishes of clients. Perhaps it has to do with human nature itself, and the fact that people with a talent for originality often have difficulty in analyzing their own particular situations and impulses.

Luckily, every rule exists only to be gracefully bent, and Albert Hadley's intelligent handling of his own apartment in New York City is the evidence at hand to prove the point—a subtly honed cluster of rooms that combine a very individual response with a very particular set of needs.

As president of Parish-Hadley, and Mrs. Parish's partner on a long series of successful design projects, he is used to wresting answers from the unresponsive fabric of Manhattan.

"My apartment is in an unremarkable building," he says, "in a pleasant, though not architecturally outstanding, neighborhood, and the view is nothing to speak of. All told, I was starting with a very familiar set of problems for the city dweller."

Albert Hadley is a gentle, modest man much given to understatement. He is spare and unaffected, and these traits are abundantly clear in the apartment he designed for himself.

"I can tell you that this apartment represents many years of accumulation," he says. "There are objects here I've inherited or been given or have bought. Now you can see what is left, even after a good deal of stringent editing. But these are the things I feel quite comfortable with. You know, one of the fascinating aspects of working in your own space is that over the years—once the initial pattern is set—individual pieces can be moved many times. I like to think of life in the same terms: as an evolution, never as something static."

But Mr. Hadley is deeply concerned with the importance of the initial pattern: "The architecture of space seems to me critical. Furniture must be placed in such a way that these dynamics are respected. Successful design depends on being honest with the basics of a room. That is not to say that I won't try to improve a bad situation, but it doesn't seem to make any sense to transform a traditionally shaped room into a contemporary one. And there's more to good design than simply filling a room with agreeable fabrics and furniture. That's only cosmetic. I'm fond of saying that 'design is total, decoration is embellishment.' To achieve the former, an intellectual eye is necessary."

Mr. Hadley reached his present enviable sense of repose after having lived through several aesthetic incarnations: "I can remember my first apartment. It was all whitewashed, with brown felt couches and horsehair chairs—and a black floor, of course. That was my no-color era. Then there was my Cecil Beaton period: all fine jewel colors. But gradually I evolved until I had enough self-realization to admit that I really preferred the happiest and most unforced of tonal values. I'm very much in favor of natural colors."

This calm understanding of a simple set of circumstances and a given repertory of needs is accurately charted in the graceful configurations of Mr. Hadley's living room.

"It's a room with a wide variety of pleasures," he comments, "from just gazing at the fire alone to being comfortable with guests."

This inherent simplicity of vision has much to do with his unique point of view. Like his personality, the space reveals itself slowly, growing in subtlety and breadth, as further dimensions are explored and brought into focus.

Recessed mirrored bases and cornices give the dark walls a floating quality. The maddening problem of how to hide heating and cooling elements was neatly solved by furring out the wall between the windows, reducing everything to a single unobtrusive grille. At the same time, this solution served to make the windows themselves deep recesses. The city is kept at an appropriate distance, and the room is given a refreshing sense of depth and solidity. A ceiling of Chinese tea paper forms a pleasant substitute for that diagram of beams so typical of the Manhattan apartment. In the same unobtrusive way, white doors slide into walls, with a discreet technological murmur. There is absolutely nothing harsh in the Hadley apartment.

He has achieved these feats of condensation—approaching invisibility—with the aid of thoughtful and structural design solutions. The entrance hall is a paradigm of this. There are no less than five different openings into this single space, but three of them are so artfully underplayed that they go unnoticed at first glance. Unnoticed, but not disguised. While there is an element of trompe l'oeil in everything Mr. Hadley does, he would not dream of cheating for the sake of any effect.

In a small apartment it is vital that each room serve multiple needs. The small studio is a good example. There is a large bulletin board—"my changeable tapestry"—and a large cushioned daybed to accommodate guests. The lighting is so designed that this very private space becomes a comfortable room for reading, as well.

"It does really come down to being truthful, doesn't it?" Mr. Hadley observes. "And it is so difficult to be completely honest with ourselves. I think we all want to do something radical and different, but the temptation should be overcome. What must be expressed is the strong continuity in the pattern of life—and our own particular preferences. A person becomes a designer because he has some intuitive flair, but he becomes a designer of merit through a long process of evolution and involvement. The eye is what needs training, through care and constant investigation."

These elegant and introspective rooms confirm the fact that Albert Hadley has conducted such trials and has reached a set of judgments in harmony with his own needs. That he could make a personal statement into a strong design solution reveals the depth of his talent. He thinks of himself as a person who—like all of us—is the product of a particular time and place and situation. And his home is what most of us would like ours to be: an inventory of experience and a symbol of personal growth and change.

The Living Room of designer Albert Hadley's Manhattan apartment contains a sophisticated mix of furnishings. BELOW LEFT: The deep-toned walls appear to float, due to their mirrored recessed cornices and bases. Subtle lighting is reflected on the Chinese tea-papered ceiling and on a 17th-century mirror framed in ebony, brass and mother-of-pearl. Furnishings and accessories are an

interesting combination of the antique and the contemporary: mid-18th-century Italian satin-covered armchairs, iron bookcases with pine shelves, a modern Japanese aluminum sculpture, a pair of Regency black-lacquered candle stands and a Portuguese painted and gilded console table whose cabriole legs terminate in miniature feet wearing high-heeled, high-topped shoes. ABOVE: Old and new objects coexist comfortably in this small, well-scaled living area. A modern plexiglass table stands on a striking 20th-century hooked rug in front of a linen-covered contemporary sofa. The base of an early 18th-century bleached pine table is carved in the shape of a crouching figure, while a 17th-century Dutch still life enhances the room's dramatic play of dark and light.

155

The small Studio serves multiple needs. ABOVE:
Though it is used as a work space, guests can be
accommodated on a cushioned daybed that conceals
another single bed. The lighting is designed so
that the room is also a pleasant place for reading.
The black-lacquered bookcase was designed in
Berlin in 1928; its gold, silver and copper
decorations depict athletic events. Sisal matting
covers the floor. OPPOSITE: Albert Hadley's unique
bulletin board—his "changeable tapestry"—is
seen above a Directoire leather-topped mahogany
writing table that, in turn, is flanked by two late-
18th-century American chairs. A chinoiserie
lacquered chest sits on the bleached oak floor.

Detail views of the Master Bedroom show Mr. Hadley's skillful combination of period pieces. ABOVE: A bull's-eye mirror from the American Federal period reflects the late-18th-century English bed and a Chinese lacquered screen. ABOVE RIGHT: A 19th-century portrait of a dog and a collection of small objects adorn a 17th-century black-lacquered chest embellished with painted scenes of the English countryside. The drawing of monolithlike forms is by Helène Fesenmaier. RIGHT: Another of Helène Fesenmaier's drawings is seen above a Regency chest. A terra-cotta bust seems to ignore a pair of iron rabbits.

A full view of the Master Bedroom includes the
lacquered bed, which is covered with a trapunto-
style bedspread and a quilt with a simple geometric
design. The designer placed a Regency draftsman's
table conveniently at his bedside, along
with two chairs from the same period. The
bleached oak flooring contributes to the
sparing yet comfortable traditional look.

# A MODERN
# PALACE IN THE
# DESERT

The inception of a dream, it is said, is often more satisfying than the fulfillment. This does not appear to be the case in the house that the late interior designer Arthur Elrod created for himself in the desert resort of Palm Springs, California.

At the beginning, the dream was surely a splendid one, but the realization of that dream is even more splendid. For together Mr. Elrod and architect John Lautner created what can only be described as a masterstroke of contemporary design. There is no other house like it, and there is probably no other setting in the world where it could be duplicated. It is a house designed with boldness and imagination, a house of dreams, a palace in the sun, a completely original concept. Whether one's reaction to it is negative or positive, superlatives must be used in discussing it. There can be no middle ground.

Literally carved out of a rocky promontory overlooking the desert south of Palm Springs, the massive form of Mr. Elrod's home is an extension of nature itself, seemingly as permanent as the San Jacinto Mountains that enfold it. Inextricably bound together, house and setting represent an outstandingly dramatic combination.

Arthur Elrod's dream started in an ordinary enough way. The design firm of which he was president has its headquarters in Palm Springs, and he wanted his home to be conveniently nearby. He also wanted to use it as a kind of second office and— most important of all—he wished to make a personal summary of his long professional experience in the field of interior design. Surely at some point in every decorator's career there occurs a compelling desire to make some ultimate personal statement, to write a clear and unmistakable signature. While working professionally for others, a designer is not often able to make—indeed, should not make—such a personal and self-indulgent gesture. But an interior designer's own house is, of course, a thoroughly different matter.

In consultation with architect Lautner, Mr. Elrod felt able to express himself completely, to give free rein to his impulses—to build the contemporary house about which he had long dreamed. The basic concept shared by architect and interior designer was that the house itself should be an integral part of the natural site chosen for its construction. This is the raison d'être of the house, the theme around which every detail revolves.

The architectural plan consists of a series of sweeping circles and curves, and the house itself seems to grow organically from rock formations and clusters of boulders. Often, in fact, the rock formations have been used to serve as interior walls. Materials chosen for construction echo the same organic theme: concrete, copper, slate, glass. The living room and master bedroom, for example, share an almost unbroken expanse of floor-to-ceiling windows, one hundred feet in length. Even the swimming pool blends gracefully into the natural setting, as water cascades over its edge down the mountainside. Interior décor reaffirms the emphasis on nature: Fabrics are rough textured, carpets are sculptured and the appropriate furniture was custom-made by the firm of Arthur Elrod Associates. Everything has been designed with a lavish hand, and in tribute to the extravagant locale, the house appears to be even larger than it really is.

What has been called "the ultimate Palm Springs house" is large, to be sure, although far from enormous. Its five rooms encompass some 5,700 square feet, but the architectural arrangement succeeds in magnifying even that generous space. The plan is a daring one, unusually irregular, and no one room is either square or rectangular. The house is divided into three large zones: an area for entertaining, a master bedroom/study and a guest room. All are arranged with the curves and outcroppings and unexpected surprises that work in harmony with the natural setting itself.

The extraordinary circular living room is a good illustration of the effects achieved by architect and interior designer. With a massive poured-concrete ceiling, the room is tentlike, sixty feet in diameter. The concrete beams on the ceiling spread out like spokes of a wheel, and the view from below suggests nothing so much as some gigantic stone flower, forever in place. Because of the mammoth fireplace and the lavish size of the room, Mr. Elrod

cleverly reduced the whole to human scale by arranging a number of different seating areas. Overwhelming though the scale may be, it is still a room in which people can relax thoroughly and be warm and comfortable and intimate.

Mr. Elrod used the same approach in the design of his large master bedroom/study. Although the room is fifty feet long, it was brought into human perspective through a number of basically simple decorative devices. The headboard of the large bed, for example, is used to divide the room, and the walls are warmly paneled in South American courbaril wood. Though the room is large, and its glass walls reveal a breathtaking panorama of mountains and natural scenery, function has been honored and intimacy achieved. To blend such contradictory elements it is necessary to have a firm understanding of the uses of space and scale.

Working in complete harmony on a project that excited them both, John Lautner and Arthur Elrod demonstrated their mastery of space and their bold concepts of design. The harmony between them was all the more remarkable, since very often an architect and an interior designer will think in quite different terms about a given project. This certainly was not the case in the creation of Mr. Elrod's Palm Springs home. In a curious way the result of the collaboration is more than simply a fine and unique house. Together Mr. Elrod and Mr. Lautner created a work of art that is an exercise in sculpture almost as much as it is an exercise in architecture and interior design.

Arthur Elrod saw his dream lavishly fulfilled, and the dream must have paled when compared with the reality. He had his magnificent eagle's nest, the great mountains surrounding him and the ever-changing colors of the desert below.

"There are so many variations possible here," Mr. Elrod observed. "Actually, in many ways it almost seems like two houses. There is the house during the day, with the mountains and the sun and the sky all around. And at night there are the lights of Palm Springs below, the stars and the moon above, and the soft lighting inside. Night and day it's a very exciting house for me."

The massive form of the Palm Springs residence of the late Arthur Elrod seems like an organic outgrowth of the surrounding rock formations and clusters of boulders at the edge of the San Jacinto Mountains. Concrete, copper, slate and glass—materials chosen for the construction by designer Elrod and architect John Lautner—form a continuous bond with the natural terrain. Floor-to-ceiling windows separate the swimming pool and terrace from the interior of the 5,700-square-foot house. Reflections of the main living area's poured-concrete beams, one of the supporting columns, and some boulders and wildflowers glisten within the placid pool. Wicker chairs comprise a seating arrangement for enjoyment of the view.

An evening view from the Pool
Terrace toward the Living Room
confirms the full impact of the
massive umbrellalike roof soaring
overhead. Spotlights spaced
regularly around the perimeter of
the 60-feet-in-diameter concrete
roof add a futuristic sense of
drama. Large sections of glass
separating the interior from the
outdoors are meticulously mitred
and joined. Where it meets natural
formations of boulders, the glass
is scribed within a fraction of an
inch to join exactly the irregular
profile of the stone. Visible are
numerous furniture groupings
designed to conform to the circular
plan of the room. On the far
wall is a large painting by
contemporary artist Paul Jenkins.

Each of the seating arrangements in the Living Room commands a different perspective of the surrounding desert and nearby mountains. The most sweeping panorama of all is from the large sofa grouping in the center of the room. The custom-designed sofa and ribbon chairs with polished chrome supports conform to the curve of a deep-pile rug textured with sculptured concentric circles; the flooring is herringbone-patterned slate. Glass-topped circular tables with plexiglass bases hold plants, small sculptures and other objects.

The Master Bedroom/Study is located in a
separate part of the structure to ensure complete
privacy. An unusual outcropping of rocks rises out
of the floor in front of a glass wall, and a
whimsical metal sculpture stands in the indoor
garden. An oversized chaise is the dominant
element of the sitting area of the suite. The
carpeting is light-toned, tightly woven goat hair.

169

# A COLORFUL AND COMPACT FAMILY APARTMENT

Interior designer Carleton Varney's interests are protean, and his energy appears to be without limit. He is president of the decorating firm of Dorothy Draper & Co., the head of a fabric house carrying his own name, the author of six books, a syndicated newspaper columnist and a sought-after lecturer in every part of the United States.

"I'm basically a worker," he explains. "I like to work, and I like the work that I am doing. It's very satisfying, and each day is truly a new and challenging experience for me."

Mr. Varney was born in Lynn, Massachusetts, and came to New York City in 1957 where he taught at a private school. Even then, however, he had begun to feel the call of another career.

"I've always been interested in decoration," he says, "and I've always studied interiors whenever and wherever I could. I knew that I had the ability to be an interior designer, but I never seemed able to get started in the right direction."

Not long after he arrived in New York, however, he managed to find a position with the Dorothy Draper firm. He began to work there in late 1959 as an assistant to Leon Hegwood, then president, and he was miraculously able to buy the company within fewer than five years.

"Having been left a little money," says Mr. Varney, "I was able to acquire stock over the years, and I was president of the company before I was thirty. At the time Mrs. Draper decided to sell, she was along in years, and no one in her immediate family wanted to carry on the business.

"I love this company, and I respect the quality of work that was started here and continues, I think, to this day. Mrs. Draper was an incredible lady, and I got along with her very well. Long ago she was using Parsons tables and plaster Baroque and geometrics. Look at the marvelous work she did for the Hampshire House, back in 1920."

Though he served his apprenticeship with Mrs. Draper, the designer has definitive ideas of his own. He was an enthusiastic student, and he has become an enthusiastic teacher.

"I don't believe in a lot of decorating rules," he says. "People should live their own lives for their own enjoyment. I don't think it's necessary to take the word of interior designers too seriously. And, really, I've made it a habit only to give suggestions.

"There's a great deal of ugliness in the world, you know. If I can help someone look at his environment and make it somehow better and more attractive to live in, then I think I've succeeded. It's because I care, you see. Caring—that would be the way to describe me."

His own eight-room apartment in New York City is a case in point. He lives there with his wife and small sons, and the apartment radiates the care and concern, not only of the professional interior designer, but of the family man as well.

"It is really a joint venture," he says. "Both my wife and I did the décor, and I really think that's the way it should be. Suzanne is my partner in the fabric business, Carleton V., too. Naturally when two people are doing the same work some compromises have to be made. I remember there was one particular room in which I wanted to use a bright yellow, and my wife wanted something rather more soft. We finally agreed on a kind of pearl gray."

It is a flexible arrangement, and it is also a most flexible way of life that the Varneys have been able to design for themselves.

"Our apartment is in a constant state of change," the designer explains. "We bought it very soon after we were married, and naturally certain changes have been inevitable. Before long, for example, the library was turned into a nursery—and so it goes. But the flexibility we are looking for is really even more basic than that.

"The dining room might be a good illustration of what I mean. We've made every effort to see that it can be used in the most fluid way possible—to be able to change the atmosphere easily to correspond with the type of entertaining we might be doing on a given night. Sometimes things are formal, sometimes very informal. We can use the table for dinners or for buffets. As a matter of fact, the dining room table is really only a folding table—nothing special, nothing elaborate, not an antique. We simply cover it with one of our fabrics. We're both fabric designers, after all."

As well as the apartment in New York—which is in a building designed by Stanford White—Mr. and Mrs. Varney have a farmhouse in Dutchess County, where they spend weekends and holidays.

"The atmosphere is exactly the same in the country," says Carleton Varney. "I don't like to throw anything away, and I like to keep changing things all the time. You know, in New York we've already done the bedroom over twice."

His professional work, however, is somewhat less free-form and flexible, though one of the continuing projects of his firm is the constant refurbishing and updating of the décor of The Greenbrier, in White Sulphur Springs. It was a vast project started by Mrs. Draper in 1946, and to this day the firm continually freshens and renovates the interiors of the famous West Virginia resort.

In addition, in the course of his career, Carleton Varney has worked for a number of well-known people. He remembers with affection, for example, his work for the late Joan Crawford. The famous actress was not quite as casual as Mr. Varney.

"Everything about her was very precise," says the designer. "This was certainly reflected in the way we worked together. For instance, when we planned a room, she would put masking tape on the floor to show where the furniture might go. She liked to walk around and sense the way a room was going to work. Joan was used to doing this on film sets—it was the way she rehearsed before the furniture was put in place."

Mr. Varney's own approach to design might be a little more flexible, it is true, but basically his impulses are the same as the ones demonstrated by Miss Crawford. He cares, and he cares enormously. He cares about the comfort and convenience of the many people for whom he works and has worked.

And perhaps that care can be seen, most personally and most informally, in the comfortable, flexible and appropriate family apartment he and his wife created on Madison Avenue. The apartment will change, the family will grow and Mr. and Mrs. Varney will be prepared for every eventuality. There are, after all, two designers in residence. What better arrangement could there be?

Designer Carleton Varney shares credit with his wife, Suzanne, for the interiors of their eight-room Manhattan apartment in a building designed by architect Stanford White. LEFT: Their productive collaboration is evident in an Oriental-inspired corner of the Living Room, here viewed through the back of a mother-of-pearl inlaid Chinese chair. Serigraph by Mr. Varney.

OPPOSITE: *A highlight of the Living Room is the colorful rug designed by Suzanne Varney. Mirrored tables reflect the rug as well as several other strong patterned fabrics. Paintings, left to right, are by Carleton Varney and Fred Hausman. Figure in foreground is by Manuel Carbonell, small table sculpture by Henry Moore.*

Large-scale patterns and floral motifs emerge once again in the Dining Room. Here—offset by white crown moldings and dado, and a pastel ceiling—a host of colorful flowers, scattered over a field of deep blue, brightens the walls. A subtle painting by Gillian Jagger echoes the soft tonalities of the moldings, ceiling and floor. In anticipation of a formal dinner party, the antique bronze lantern gleams, and candles glow in stately French bronze candelabras. Tables draped with moiré cloths relate to the long, contemporary lacquered console; delicate gold-painted ballroom chairs await the arrival of guests. An intricately faceted antique Venetian mirror above a leather-and-mirror server captures a reflection of the lantern. The painted and stenciled hardwood floor repeats elements from the wallcovering and adds a trellis pattern.

Flowers bloom in the Master Bedroom,
where a painting of roses by Ted-Seth Jacobs
is reflected in an ornate gilded mirror. A
delicate floral print covering the painted
Louis XV armchair and bench, and the
draped bedside table, accents the sunbright
walls and carpet, and contrasts with the
tailored canopy bed. Hand-appliquéd
garlands adorn the bed linens, while a
Bristol bedside lamp furthers the floral motif.

# HOTEL

# PENTHOUSE

# ON

# NOB HILL

"I'm something of a chameleon," says interior designer Eleanor Ford of San Francisco. "Whatever the person I'm working for is, I tend to become."

Certainly she has strong convictions of her own, but she feels that her responsibility is to respect the wishes of her clients—particularly in the matter of style and period. She herself is fully at home and comfortable working in both the traditional and the contemporary genre.

When Cyril Magnin, businessman and philanthropist, acquired his new apartment in San Francisco, he first considered using traditional décor. But on a trip to London he studied English and French period furniture with greater care—and hesitated. Then one day he happened to see and acquire a large and extremely bold contemporary tapestry by artist Mark Adams, and the matter of décor was, from that moment, settled in his mind.

Called *The Great Wing*, the tapestry provides the decorative key to the entire apartment. Its brilliant colors, covering almost an entire wall of the living room, demand a deliberately subdued background to set it off properly. And Eleanor Ford provided throughout the apartment what she refers to as "a pure classical backdrop for art."

"People are inclined to make themselves old because they think old," says Cyril Magnin. "I certainly don't and I'm sure my apartment reflects that point of view. I feel extremely comfortable here. At first I was going to buy a condominium, but fortunately my daughter convinced me that this would be a better solution. And it is."

Perhaps what is most unusual about the apartment is its location, on the fifteenth floor of the Mark Hopkins Hotel, on San Francisco's Nob Hill. It is not at all large, containing only an entrance hall, a living room, bedroom and bath, a library/dining room, an atrium and a small compact kitchen.

Most of the original hotel décor was soon eliminated. Interior designer Ford quickly removed a false fireplace and pink velvet walls and instead found solutions more appropriate to Mr. Magnin's collections of primitive and contemporary art. She committed herself, as Mr. Magnin had, to a theme of classical simplicity.

Marble was brought in from Tennessee for the floors. Called "Tennessee pink," its color is more nearly a warm beige and was given a soft matte finish rather than a highly polished one. Carpeting was specially woven in Puerto Rico to match the marble, and Eleanor Ford covered the walls in a similar shade of linen, a color repeated in lamp shades as well as Roman shades. The same color range is also found in two large sofas of oyster-hued leather, pieces so large that they had to be constructed in sections so that they could fit into the hotel elevator and be brought up to the fifteenth floor.

The emphasis everywhere is on the owner's art collections. A ledge behind the sofas, for example, was built to hold such objects as carved wooden impala heads, which were formerly used as head-dresses, and other African statuary.

The designer also provided unobtrusive recessed lighting to illuminate favorite pieces of art: a Vasica, for example, and a collage by Bruno Chase. Curiously enough, even the view from the outside provides a form of art, and through one of the windows appears something that looks very much like a large pre-Columbian stone carving or an exotic pyramid. It is, in fact, simply part of the hotel's exterior architecture.

Comfort and function are honored throughout the apartment. The short tables in front of the living room sofas are covered in lacquered laminated plastic and are practically indestructible. Linen-covered pedestals do double duty, holding lamps as well as concealing hidden stereo speakers.

Three steps up from the living room is the atrium, which Eleanor Ford transformed from a small and quite useless terrace into a delightful and practical space. It is now entirely enclosed in glass, warm and cozy even in the most inclement weather. Furniture is wrought iron, and chairs are covered in vinyl because of exposure to the sun. Baskets of plants provide graceful accents and suggest the indoor/outdoor emphasis of the area.

Three steps down, on the other side of the atrium, is a small library lined with bookshelves, and there is a dramatic view of San Francisco Bay below. In addition to books the shelves hold many small and treasured objects, including gifts from the sister of the shah of Iran. The library also serves as a dining room, and it is here that Mr. Magnin entertains small groups for breakfast or luncheon. The designer has provided once more the appropriate background and furnishings for the room's dual purpose. The round table and bookcases are made of white mountain oak, and the chairs are Queen Anne, some originals and some reproductions, bleached and covered in vinyl.

There is a small bar and a tiny kitchen, but almost no cooking is done in the apartment. When entertaining, Mr. Magnin simply calls room service. It is, understandably, difficult to remember that this is a hotel apartment. But the owner often has large cocktail parties, and as many as a hundred people can be accommodated comfortably in the living room, library and atrium—if a bit snugly. For a larger party Mr. Magnin is in the habit of taking over one of the hotel's public rooms.

"Actually the living room does need a lot of people to bring it to life," says the designer. "But the bedroom is something else again. I think that it really is very cozy and personal."

More than this, the bedroom is the nerve center of the whole apartment. It contains direct telephone lines and all the other accoutrements of the busy executive. But in addition it is a warm and pleasant room, and its warmth derives in large measure from tables covered with photographs of family and friends, and from the magical window through which the owner can see a view of his beloved San Francisco Bay the first thing in the morning and the last thing in the evening.

Thus Eleanor Ford and Mr. Magnin have created a very personal apartment in an unusual context on the top of Nob Hill. The apartment is a contemporary statement, geared at once to business and pleasure, to art and the spectacular natural setting of San Francisco. It is a design that looks very much to the future, not because the designer insisted upon that dispensation, but rather because it reflects the wishes of the owner.

"I would like to die young," says Cyril Magnin. "Young in my thinking, that is."

Designer Eleanor Ford created "a pure classical backdrop for art" for Mr. Cyril Magnin's apartment in San Francisco's Mark Hopkins Hotel. OPPOSITE: In the Entrance Hall, an African queen sculpture, a steel construction by James Prestini and a Siamese mask establish a gallerylike atmosphere. BELOW: Mark Adams's tapestry The Great Wing dominates a wall of the Living Room.

Other Living Room views reveal matte-finished "Tennessee pink" marble brought specially from that state for the floors and a rug woven in Puerto Rico to match. African and pre-Columbian sculptures occupy a ledge behind the sofas, and a Vasica painting provides an abstract backdrop. On another wall, a Bruno Chase collage offsets a gleaming Jean Arp sculpture.

LEFT: *The skull of a Scottish mountain ram and the glazed terra-cotta pilasters of the Atrium frame the entrance to the Library/Dining Room. The round table and lacquer-trimmed, built-in bookcases of the dual-purpose room are of white mountain oak; the set of Queen Anne chairs was bleached to match.* BELOW LEFT: *Raised three steps higher than the living room and the library/dining room, the Atrium was formerly an open terrace. Designer Ford transformed it into an all-weather space by completely enclosing it with glass, and she used vinyl-cushioned wrought iron furniture to make it sun-proof. The outstanding view of the city includes an exotic pyramidlike structure, which is actually a parapet of the Mark Hopkins.*

# A DESIGNER'S ECLECTIC WEEKEND RETREAT

There is an exuberant and unstudied air about the weekend retreat William Pahlmann has arranged for himself in the country, some fifty miles from New York City. Mr. Pahlmann is a well-known interior designer, but the nineteenth-century carriage house he rents on an estate in Pound Ridge is quite unlike the work he is in the habit of doing for others. First of all, he was able to do more or less as he wished, and the carriage house—actually a barn in form and size—allows him any number of highly personal and unrestrained indulgences.

From the beginning, the barn, rented from old friends, had innumerable advantages. Furnishings that were already in the carriage house were more than adequate: chairs, tables, large comfortable sofas and a many-branched chandelier that conformed to the large space and appealed to his sense of drama. There were other advantages, too.

"The enormous sweep of the old rough-wood walls, which vault to the ridgepole," he says, "challenged me with the kind of space I rarely have at my command. The challenge was irresistible!"

He spent a good portion of the first summer "clinging perilously," in his words, to an elongated extension ladder, hanging favorite objects he had been keeping in storage. These included several dozen American paintings, both traditional and contemporary, and a large collection of antique porcelain platters and chargers, ranging from Chinese Export and Dutch Delft to French faïence and English ironstone. The effect of the fine old porcelain and the paintings against the rough weathered wood of the barn walls pleased Mr. Pahlmann so much that he soon found himself swept up in an extensive design project. He began searching for other striking and appropriate effects with which he could still further enhance the lofty spaces.

"I began to brood about the massive chimney breast of rosy old brick above the marvelous fireplace that can accommodate a full-size tree trunk," he says. "After the brooding was over, I hung a vast historical painting over it at a rakish slant, and below I posed an old figurehead from a ship. The figurehead is a demure and virginal lady—possibly Jenny Lind—dressed in blue, and I attached her to the chimney breast with sturdy black chains. Now she leans out into the room just as if she were attached to the prow of a ship."

As a result of the designer's exuberance and the multitude of objects he had in storage, all available wall space was soon filled, even in the large living room. But there were other problems to tackle. In frustration he turned his attention to the floor. He placed handbraided area rugs in front of the hearth, and then somehow he felt that this called for the use of a large, round, antique Chinese table he had in storage. Surrounded with stools, the table now provides a marvelous space for books and magazines, for games and informal meals. The effect having pleased him, one thing led to another, and objects once more came tumbling out of his storage vaults in generous profusion. He brought to Pound Ridge eight Chinese chairs and a seventeenth-century English refectory table he had on hand. It seemed inevitable that two favorite rosewood cabinets would be used for storing silver and linen.

More and more caught up in the project, Mr. Pahlmann was not even satisfied with the Pandora's box of his own he had opened. He found in an antiques shop—and naturally could not resist buying them—eight overscaled Russian brass candlesticks that burn big fat white candles. By this time there did not seem to be much more room to add anything else, so the designer raised his eyes in desperation to the ceiling. There he noticed that the rafters above a two-story window were miraculously bare. Somehow, with the help of his ever-present extension ladder, he managed to set a bamboo pole among the rafters and hang from it a pair of scarlet embroidered Chinese banners, which now wave gracefully in the soft summer breeze and provide a note of color year round. Even then there was still room for a bright contemporary rug beneath the large chandelier, and in a final gesture Mr. Pahlmann managed to squeeze in two Italian blackamoor statues to flank the doorway to the bedroom.

Undaunted, the designer began to look for other space to fill. He turned his attention to a large loft, reached by a double stairway from the living room. Here he created a small area of privacy, with a work table—although he exclaims that during that period "I didn't seem to have time to do any!"—some rattan daybeds, different types of chairs and two large, fanciful poufs made from a pair of Oriental rugs. He also made use of an old feed bin from the time when the barn had truly been a barn.

"The interior," William Pahlmann comments, "is either a triumph of eclecticism or an example of the interior designer run amok, depending upon how you look at it. To be frank, I really don't care. I love it, and that's really what matters in any interior. I think the place is comfortable and amusing, and it has a very relaxing effect on me—and, I believe, on my weekend guests as well."

At last the day came when even Mr. Pahlmann's exuberance, the resources of his storage vaults and the size of the barn gave out. He saw that the task was finished and that there was nothing else he really needed or could even justify adding—though necessity was surely never one of his guiding principles in this particular instance.

"I was so pleased with the whole thing," he says, "that I decided to honor my landlords with a party to express my gratitude. I suppose I didn't exercise any particular sense of proportion or control with the party, either.

"I banked the living area with masses of shaggy yellow chrysanthemums and converted the three-car garage into a discothèque, decorating it with a canopy of wildly colorful sheets by Emilio Pucci. There were amusing posters on the wall, a platform for dancing, a long bar and a series of tables for four, covered with brightly colored cloths. We had a marvelous time. At least, I did!"

Mr. Pahlmann's enthusiasm is infectious, and the charm of his new country retreat undeniable.

"If there is any practical application to my 'barnstorming,'" he says, "it is that a basic attention to scale and proportion and comfort are about the only rules you have to follow in planning an interior. And I mean any interior. Rigid rules make rigid rooms, and I'm not interested in something static and inhibited. Believe me, if you like it, then it's correct. So let yourself go! Certainly that's what I've done here in Pound Ridge."

William Pahlmann's Westchester County
country retreat—a converted 19th-century barn/
carriage house—retains its original raftered and
beamed ceilings, rough walls and wide wood-
planked floors. The designer chained an
antique ship's figurehead to the Living Room's
used-brick chimney breast and angled a large
historical painting high above it.

A variety of collectables personalizes the rustic atmosphere of the Dining Area. RIGHT: Antique Chinese chairs surround a narrow Jacobean table. The bar is made from old barn siding; above it is an American primitive painting. BELOW RIGHT: The wall space is filled with a large collection of antique porcelain platters and chargers, ranging from Chinese Export and Dutch Delft to French faïence and English ironstone, interspersed with Indian and American paintings. A pair of Chinese embroidered banners hang from the rafters. OPPOSITE: Another view reveals the double stairway to the loft and the skylight area of the vaulted, three-story-high ceiling. A pair of Italian blackamoors flank a doorway to the bedrooms.

*Mr. Pahlmann designed the Loft to fill the need
for privacy when he uses it as an office. It also
offers a more intimate environment within the vast
space for entertaining small groups or for
accommodating overnight guests. The Chinese
screen backdrops a Louis XV porter's chair and a
Chinese garden stool. Porcelain platters, drawings
and a carriage lamp add visual appeal.*

*The versatile sitting/sleeping area of the Loft is appointed with rattan daybeds and Indonesian drum tables. An antique Chinese wood figure presides graciously from a travertine-topped table, which is surrounded by early-19th-century American painted chairs. The tones of the floral-patterned Chinese rug are restated by a Chinese jardinière and a pair of opaline lamp bases.*

# A
# VICTORIAN APARTMENT
# UPDATED

The setting is an old Victorian mansion in San Francisco, converted into apartments during World War II. Today the original living room and dining room of the old house constitute one apartment, the home of Anthony Machado, a young Californian whose star is rising in the interior design world. The original pantry has been turned into a bathroom, and part of the living room has become the kitchen.

"Actually," says Mr. Machado, "I didn't make many changes; the structural beauty was here from the beginning, and I have what is the best part of the house. The height of the ceilings and the handsome moldings are incredible. There are two marble fireplaces, and it's marvelous when they're both going, in the winter. During the day it's a very comfortable place, but I think it's really an evening apartment. At night it's very magical for me."

The magic is more than understandable, since the young designer has many fascinating objects with which to conjure up innumerable effects.

"They're things I've picked up traveling," he says. "The celadon vases above the fireplace, for example, were excavated from archaeological diggings at Laguna in the Philippines. And I designed the mirror and had the frame with its plant and animal imagery needlepointed in Kashmir.

"Naturally everything in the apartment is a part of me. It was all selected with love and it shows what I'm all about, I suppose. Nothing was bought just to fill a particular spot but rather, because it meant something to me. So, in a sense, the apartment is my portrait, a record of my taste, my life, my interests and even of my feelings. Certainly that's why it works, in my opinion."

It works so well, in fact, that the apartment itself is very close to being seductive. It seems to entice the guest to enter, to sink down into a sofa—to stay just a little longer.

"I really think the sign of a successful interior," says the designer, "is when people come in and want to stay. And people do seem to feel comfortable here. There's nothing alien about it.

"You know, I've been in so many interiors that are cold and rigid, that make you want to get up and leave. That sort of approach may be fine for a showroom, where you only want to visualize something, but it's not what living is all about. It has absolutely nothing to do with making personal space comfortable and appropriate. Living is really what interior design is all about.

"Take this apartment, for example. It really wasn't designed in any coherent way. It just sort of happened bit by bit. There was a Swedish table I had had for years, and it seemed to fit in. I had some favorite mirrors, and then I found an interesting sofa fabric, a fabric that seemed to establish some sort of theme. So one thing simply led to another.

"The whole idea of decorating, it seems to me, is putting a diversity of things together and making them work. I will admit it was something of a struggle here to achieve this coherence, since there are many odd things around. There was a lot of balancing to be done. But anything can work, if it's balanced properly—colors, textures, shapes.

"And I didn't have the problems or the decisions to make that I generally have when I design for others: no floor plans, no fabric samples, no elaborate plans. In a way, there's no logic to this particular apartment, no reason or formula. It's eclectic, and I've only used the things that mean something to me. But the mixture doesn't bother me at all. I think that any well-designed and beautiful piece will go with any other, no matter what the period or style. Inevitably, it's all going to work."

Surely it is not quite as simple as he makes it sound. Anthony Machado began collecting, and also started his career as an interior designer, almost as soon as he was out of school. But one day on an impulse he decided that he had to see something of the world. With this in mind, he sold everything and bought some airplane tickets.

"For a while I thought I'd settle someplace in the south of Europe," he says, "and paint. The Bohemian life of the artist sounded very glamorous to me. As it turned out, I began my travels in Japan and went on to India and Bali and Indonesia— collecting things as I went along."

His passion for collecting soon reduced the funds he had set aside for the Bohemian life, and he decided to move to New York and begin painting

seriously. After a short time, he came to San Francisco, which he now calls home.

"I enjoy painting very much," he says. "But for me it's more difficult and draining than work in interior design. So I go from one to the other. The arrangement seems successful.

"Actually, interior design is not that different from painting, and there are many similarities. I like the tactile feeling of painting, and I like the visual arts in general. For me it's very difficult to separate the two disciplines. If I limit myself to interior designing, I feel vaguely dissatisfied and empty. So I have to paint. Yet if I did nothing but paint, I think I would be dead before I was thirty, since it takes so much out of me. But I do manage to put one of my paintings in almost every interior I design. It has become sort of a trademark of mine."

But Mr. Machado's first concern in any interior is its connection with people. They are the most important aspects of any interior, he feels.

"The environment shouldn't overpower you," he says. "It should be developed to bring out the best in people, to make them feel comfortable and at home. A room cannot be considered simply for itself, for some abstract elegance of design. I don't think interior design—or painting, for that matter— has any validity without the human element. That's why my apartment is so very personal. I couldn't have it any other way. It has to express me.

"A friend of mine said he found this apartment unusual, because it has no identifiable feeling of locale. It might be in New York or San Francisco—or someplace in Europe. Well, that's really the point, I think. It could be anywhere at any time, and nothing will go out of style really. That's because the apartment is an expression of me, not of any particular time or locale.

"All of this is part of the great responsibility of the designer, I think. If you're going to create an environment for anybody else, you have to have a very honest opinion of yourself, a good deal of self-knowledge. You have to know what you are, first of all. That's what I've tried to do here. I think I've succeeded on a purely personal level, and it's the basic first step in interior design."

The Entrance Hall of Anthony
Machado's small apartment in a
converted Victorian mansion in
San Francisco draws its primary
inspiration from the Orient,
where the youthful designer has
traveled widely. Four deep-
hued Chinese sang de boeuf vases
seem to float on plexiglass
boxes, while an orchid-filled bowl
rests solidly on a Chinese
lacquered chest. The lacquered
mirror frame is also Chinese, and
the woven matting that
textures the walls is Japanese.

*Suffused with the warm glow of firelight, the
Living Room features a versatile glass-topped, deer
antler-based table. Repeating the animal motif
are an 18th-century Japanese screen with heron
imagery, two Louis XV chairs upholstered in
spotted fawn and a lacquered goat from Thailand.
Contributing a spiritual aura is (see* DETAIL*) a
benign Japanese polychromed monk.*

OPPOSITE: *Gracing a corner of the Living Room, an 18th-century Swedish table supports a mélange of objects: Chinese jars, leather-bound volumes, a silver candlestick, a prickly cactus and a pair of French mercury-coated globes. Above the table is a mirror whose frame Mr. Machado designed and had needlepointed in Kashmir. In the foreground is a pair of plump slipper chairs.*

ABOVE: *Exuberant plants frame a Living Room sofa upholstered in swirling, marblelike fabric softened with fringe. Balancing each other, at either end of the sofa, are an African-inspired wood table and a 1930s plaster spiral standing lamp. Resting on the muted Indian durrie rug is a chrome-trimmed translucent table adorned with cactus and an oddly shaped Japanese lacquered ostrich-leg candlestick. Deliberately eclectic, the room reflects the designer's belief that "anything can work, if it's balanced properly."*

ABOVE: *The Master Bedroom, like the living room, enjoys the impressive architectural detailing that distinguished the original Victorian mansion: a high, heavily beamed ceiling, graceful moldings and a marble fireplace. These features are dramatized by beams and moldings that were painted to contrast with the walls and ceiling, and by the use of unelaborate Roman shades. In harmony with the rest of the apartment, the room is a subtle mixture of neutral tones and muted accents, of simplified contemporary furniture, tall potted plants and exotic Oriental objets d'art.*

ABOVE: *A painter as well as an interior designer, Anthony Machado included one of his works, a collage of birch trees in winter, in the Master Bedroom. Centered above the bed, it functions as another window.* LEFT: *Since the apartment is rented, the designer chose to avoid extensive structural changes. He created an interesting architectural framework for the Master Bathroom by using one trompe l'oeil wallpaper that approximates marble and another that resembles a three-dimensional cornice. A marble-topped sink, crystal chandelier, Lucite wall unit and Redouté monkey prints complete the effect.*

# FRANK
# LLOYD WRIGHT
# REVISITED

One of the primary definitions of the creative genius must be *uniqueness*. A sensibility that carries a vision to reality may fuse different elements into ultimate coherence, but it remains inimitable. Yet every great innovator has had a number of devoted followers who have not understood this and who have tried to broaden and deepen another's personal vision. It is seldom successful.

When Mrs. Martin A. Fisher acquired a Frank Lloyd Wright house, one of a relative handful in New York State, she wisely skirted such a trap by commissioning John Saladino to update and revitalize the interiors, where necessary. Mr. Saladino is hardly a follower of anyone, and he has earned a reputation as a leading young American interior designer in his own right.

Built in 1955, the house came late in Frank Lloyd Wright's adventurous career. But it is inclined to echo his "Prairie Houses" of the first decade of this century, with its deep eaves, *L*-shaped plan and horizontal massing. Upon buying the house some twenty years later, Mrs. Fisher realized that some additions were required. Always keeping in mind the sense of integrity and continuity she owed the architect who had created her house, she traveled to visit Mrs. Wright herself to discuss the project.

The result was the new wing Mrs. Fisher added in 1972. It was designed by architect Morton Delson, who had been associated with Frank Lloyd Wright at *Taliesin* and who had been the project manager of the house when it was built originally. Mr. Delson used the same sort of materials that had gone into the original building: stone, plaster and cedar shakes. The new composition is calm and sober, and echoes Wright's basic premise that a house, both interior and exterior, must be a complete unit with a coherent flow from inside to outside. In this matter there were, of course, consultations between Mr. Delson and Mr. Saladino. Though they seemed on the surface to represent different schools of thought, there was little conflict, but instead, a pleasurable cooperation.

"It never worried me that I might be altering the work of a master," says Mr. Saladino. "On the contrary, I tried to maintain the integrity of his design—but within my own frame of reference. Personally my ideas are rather more rooted in the Bauhaus tradition, in the styles of the 1920s. I like walls that are mirrored to extend space, and columns that dissolve in reflections of stainless steel."

Thus, John Saladino would seem to have a late-twentieth-century sensibility in some ways incompatible with Frank Lloyd Wright's own. It is a tribute to both an old and a new sensibility that the work of interior redesigning went so well.

As is typical of so many other Wright designs, the house itself seems to grow organically out of the landscape and to flow effortlessly from exterior through interior and out again. Mr. Saladino, however, did have some reservations about the plan of the large central living room.

"The view of the water, a very fine one, was in a way ignored," he explains. "All the original emphasis seemed to center on the fireplace. It reminded me of some Medieval fortress in the north of Europe, with its life built around a great hearth. And here I came, like some Renaissance Italian, bursting onto the scene and bringing my Mediterranean preoccupation with light and air and color!"

But it is important to remember that Mrs. Fisher's needs had changed the direction of the original Frank Lloyd Wright design. She was using the house as a summer home, not as an all-year residence. This serves to explain certain of the readjustments Mr. Saladino had to make—readjustments like turning the view away from the fireplace and bringing the summer and the surrounding landscape more positively into the house.

"Do you know how I did it?" he asks. "By contrasting monumental scale with transparent color. I knew at once that I couldn't use pure white. It would be just too much in these rooms. So I worked out a program based on cream and a cool gray, with some peach tones. These are highly contemporary colors but still compatible with the original Wrightian concept."

The selection of furniture proved yet another challenge for the young designer. The house had been bought furnished, and it contained a rather erratic collection. "There were pieces by Wright freely mixed with what we might call early *Gemütlich*," says Mr. Saladino. "And there were any number of nineteenth-century Chinese things that didn't belong at all under any circumstances."

Most of the original pieces designed by Wright himself were salvaged, however, although John Saladino severely edited the architect's penchant for built-in bookcases. Those that he did retain were given an extra dimension with mirror backing. Central to his working method was a lack of inhibition about modifying and revitalizing work when he felt it necessary. There were excitements, too, that accompanied this unusual design assignment.

"Treasures kept appearing as we went along," says the designer. "For example, we found an original mahogany Wright table in the caretaker's apartment. There was also a wing table that Wright had designed to wrap around a column. I added a fourth wing, then we put it in a different location."

Mr. Saladino's pleasurable relationship with the past, and his joy in the assignment, nevertheless do not seem to interfere with a lively critical dialogue he appears to have taken up with the Wrightian sensibility. It is not arrogance; it is simply that his point of view was molded by other forces.

"But I learned to control them," says Mr. Saladino. "And while I didn't approach the project as if I were a museum curator, I think I managed to successfully bridge the gap between restoration and updating. My own feelings about design are more concerned with the shape of space and objects and the relation they have to human beings. I think of environments as divine landscapes."

It is more than doubtful that Frank Lloyd Wright would have used such terminology, but there is an ease and coherence in the way that John Saladino's lively use of color responds to the dynamic of the master's spaces.

There is every possibility that Wright himself would have given a nod of satisfaction and approval, perhaps grudgingly, to a sometimes irreverent, but always vital, experiment in reclaiming the spirit—if not the exact substance—of the past. The house was a work of art originally and, refreshed and refurbished, it remains so.

The mahogany, glass and stone façade of this distinctive Frank Lloyd Wright house, built in 1955 in New York State, commands a panoramic bayfront view. When Mrs. Martin A. Fisher acquired the residence in 1972, she asked designer John Saladino to revitalize the interiors. The L-shaped plan of the structure was modified that year by architect Morton Delson.

Restored flagstone Living Room flooring extends to
the terraces, linking the house with the
landscape. The major seating unit, a custom-
designed L-shaped sofa, focuses on the ocean view.
A lightly scaled wicker chair completes the
conversation group, defined by a Russian wolf area
rug. An Oriental drum and a primitive stone
sculpture serve as tables.

BELOW: *Sections of the original cabinetwork were removed and replaced with a colorful high-backed banquette in one corner of the Living Room. Lacquered panels were placed between the original mahogany shelves, and an incandescent light strip was concealed under each shelf. The mahogany-and-glass clerestory area, a familiar Wrightian element, is interrupted by plants.*

LOWER LEFT: *A skylight illuminates the Card Room's vivid lacquered paneling, banquette and carpet. Inasmuch as this room was originally the kitchen, the two lighted sculpture niches once housed wall ovens.*
LOWER RIGHT: *Pre-Columbian kneeling and crouching figures survey the Dining Room, with its light furnishings and silk-wrapped wall panels. Recessed lighting dramatizes both rooms.*

203

BELOW: *In one of the Bedrooms, a mirrored backing was added to Frank Lloyd Wright's built-in bookcases, providing an extra dimension; all shelving and mahogany paneling is original. Sheets of bronze mirror above the paneled walls meet the pitched ceiling. The carpeting continues on the wall behind the bed and the Oriental lacquered bedside tables. Plant-filled baskets accent the room.*

RIGHT: *Gradations of a monochromatic color scheme achieve an understated look in another Bedroom. Bronze mirroring above a silk-paneled wall visually extends the pitched ceiling. The bench at the foot of the bed is wrapped in the same carpeting that covers the floor.*

Blending with the surrounding landscape, an
exterior view of the residence emphasizes its
uncompromising horizontality. Visible is the new
wing that was added by Taliesin Associated
Architects using stone, plaster and cedar shakes—
materials similar to those that had gone into the
original building.

# A LEGENDARY COTTAGE IN HOLLYWOOD

An aura of romantic legend surrounds the house. Names once associated with the estate of which it was a part—King Vidor, Eleanor Boardman, Dolores Costello, John Barrymore—recall a vanished era of bravura, opulence and extravagant gesture. These names are certainly among the most glamorous and evocative in the Hollywood mythology of the 1920s and the early 1930s.

North of Sunset Boulevard in Beverly Hills, the house was one of several built in 1925 on a six-acre estate by film director King Vidor. The main house itself was appropriately baronial, and some years later it appealed to the elaborate tastes of John Barrymore, who bought it after he married Dolores Costello. That lordly and magnificent actor added a fuller measure of splendor—pools and fountains and a series of smaller houses. Over the years, however, the glamour faded, the extravagant gestures became faint memories and through death and attrition the estate fell into decay.

When John Calley, head of production at a Hollywood film studio, bought one of the small houses on an acre of the large estate, his motives were two-fold. He saw the potential of the house, and, a filmmaker himself, he more than appreciated the rich echoes of Hollywood history it contained. A bachelor, he felt the house would be ideal for him—small, private, graced with a magnificent setting and filled with memories of the past.

But Mr. Calley is a busy man. He needed help to repair the ravages of time and to create a comfortable background for his life. So he called upon Los Angeles interior designer Leonard Stanley for the necessary advice and alterations.

"I can only give you a general idea of what I like," he told Mr. Stanley. "Frankly, I don't have the time to go into a great deal of detail."

He and the designer proceeded to pore over art books and photographs of interiors until they had reached a rather amorphous understanding of the direction the décor and restoration would take. The flexibility of the arrangement quite naturally appealed to Leonard Stanley.

"Mr. Calley gave me what amounted to carte blanche," he explains. "Frankly, this is the most freedom I've ever had on a project. But in many ways I think it's the ideal situation. After all, the main part of being an effective designer—a professional designer, if you wish—is to be able to put yourself into someone else's frame of reference. I am glad that the owner allowed me to do more or less what I wanted, and the fact that he was pleased with the eventual result does add credence to my point of view and sensibility."

Initially there was a great deal to be done. Even though the house was small—and largely *because* the house was small—extensive renovation and redesign were required. There were innumerable immediate problems to be solved.

"Potentially charming," says Mr. Stanley, "this small house was very difficult to decorate. First of all, when Mr. Calley bought the place, it was almost a complete wreck inside. No one had touched or bothered about anything for years, and the whole atmosphere reeked of disintegration. Secondly, and most important, was the matter of dimensions. It wasn't simply that the house was small. It was the fact that windows and doors were all in exactly the wrong places, and the shape of many of the rooms was unbelievably awkward.

"Take the living room, for example. Really, you can't even call it a living room—more of a gallery; thirty feet long and twelve feet wide. When you open the front door, you almost fall into the fireplace. It gave me some headaches."

His solutions, however, were sweeping and conclusive. He refurbished neglected ceiling beams, added a large amount of wood paneling, closed up improbable windows and doors and added—in the bedrooms particularly—generous French doors and balconies to take advantage of lovely vistas, until then almost entirely sealed away from view.

More difficult were the problems involved in dealing with rooms of odd shape and dimension. His solution was one that is characteristic of his design work in general, one requiring a firm understanding of the nature of scale. He filled the small rooms of Mr. Calley's house with overscaled furniture and bold fabrics. To the amateur, such a treatment might appear eccentric or unreasonable.

"Perhaps it does seem paradoxical," Mr. Stanley concedes. "But I feel strongly that a small room, in particular, requires large furniture and dramatic fabrics. It's my personal taste, I will admit, but I also think it's a valid principle of design. It seems to work well in this small space, and you can certainly have a very busy room, and at the same time give a peaceful and uncrowded effect."

The furniture is large, and the fabrics are bold, sometimes intrusive. But Mr. Stanley is quite correct: Such a treatment serves to enlarge, rather than to diminish. This manipulation of space, and the reconciliation of conflicting elements, could easily have been a disaster in amateur hands. Though the treatment is characteristic of much of Leonard Stanley's other work, he rejects out of hand the idea of any kind of design signature.

"Surely a designer will have a few trademarks," he says. "But when you walk into a house, the initial impact must come from the personality of the house itself and from the personality of the owner. Certainly it should not come from the decorator. Part of being an effective interior designer is the ability to put yourself in someone else's head, to think and choose just as he would."

And personality is the strong feature of the Calley home. When fog drifts in from the ocean, the small English-style country house seems remote, adrift and mysterious. The setting is somehow dramatic and theatrical, miniature as it may be. It generates a feeling quite in keeping with the illustrious history of the house itself.

The echoes of the past are stronger now, the days of John Barrymore more vivid, the glamour restored in small measure. And there is the additional excitement of a newer Hollywood mythology. In the screening room, which the designer created over the garage, are the images of a more contemporary mythology: favorite photographs of Humphrey Bogart, portraits from *The Maltese Falcon* and *Casablanca* and the other films.

Continuity and tradition have been restored, if a trifle simplified, and a house that had been allowed to decay—though alive with memories—has been given an appealing rebirth.

BELOW: *Two late-17th-century painted dummy-board figures of children welcome visitors into the Living Room of filmmaker John Calley's Hollywood cottage. The balanced arrangement includes pairs of studded screens, side tables with bouillotte lamps, and potted ferns. The spotted dog in an 18th-century painting echoes the cowhide upholstery on the Louis XV fireside furnishings.*

OPPOSITE: *After completing a major restoration, designer Leonard Stanley found he had a number of spatial problems to solve; unifying the long narrow Living Room was his initial task. The solution was to symmetrically repeat furnishings and fabric patterns. Two large Louis XV chairs, unusually covered in black-and-white cowhide, face each other. Two sofas, also with a deliberately overscaled pattern, balance each other on either side of the antique carved-wood front door. Cannister lamps flank the sofas, and large Louis XV suede-covered stools stand in front of the lamp tables. The use of skins continues with a rug of deep-toned Norwegian cowhides. The designer's choice of large dramatic furnishings, coupled with the rustic beams and wood floors, creates a rugged country look—exactly what John Calley wanted for his bachelor digs.*

The Screening Room was added over the garage
after Mr. Calley acquired the residence. A tailored
tartan fabric covers the walls, draperies, sofa,
armchairs and floor pillows. A variety of
contrasting plaids covers cushions, two rush-seat
chairs and a small bench. Photographs of
Humphrey Bogart, whom Mr. Calley admired,
conceal apertures for projection equipment.

ABOVE: In the rustic setting of the beamed Master Bedroom, the vivid pattern for walls, bedcovering and draperies contrasts effectively with the solid-color canopy lining, upholstered headboard, stool and pleated lamp shades. French doors open to a view of the garden. LEFT: An antique carved-wood bear grasping a mirror, which serves as a towel rack, adds an amusing touch to the Bathroom. The wood-mounted bathtub is further enhanced by marble.

# A STYLE

# FOR

# SEASIDE LIVING

"It's neither a Fire Island beach house nor an apple-green and white country cottage," says Michael de Santis. "And it's not stark, stark modern—which most people don't really like anyway."

The interior designer is describing the Long Island house he decorated for himself and later sold to a friend, who keeps everything from paintings to dinner plates exactly as Mr. de Santis left them. Nothing was changed. Nothing had to be.

This is a tribute to the sure hand of the interior designer. But perhaps it is also a tribute to the new owner, since half the pleasure of buying a new house often derives from changing the old décor completely. The owner, however, recognized that Michael de Santis had managed with an elegant sense of the appropriate, to create a house exactly in keeping with Long Island and its role as a leading resort area in the United States.

Starting with a fine waterside lot—but with a small, unprepossessing house moved by former owners from a neighboring farm—Mr. de Santis turned the property into a splendid summer complex. It is now complete with boat slip, tennis court, poolside dining pavilion and greenhouse—a lovely carefree world of its own.

Having no interiors that were worth preserving, the original house was virtually dissolved and replaced with free-flowing additions that open one from another, with an easy relaxed movement of unconfined volumes and perspectives.

The designer's sense of volumes indeed appears to be somewhat unique. He solves problems in a highly individual way. There was in the house, for example, an unlikely bathroom whose proportions were six by twenty-six feet. Many another designer would have shortened this anomaly or widened it, if not abandoned it completely. Quite undaunted, Mr. de Santis extended the length of the room even farther by adding a small courtyard/garden beyond a glassed-in bathtub. Then he mirrored the long walls to reflect an assertively geometric carpet and gleaming metallic ceiling paper. The strongly reflected patterns transform what was formerly a drab hallway and bathroom into a dynamic open space—bright, animated and inviting.

Ceiling treatments are another of the designer's special talents. Rather than unifying the diverse procession of original rooms and additions with the clean sweep of flat ceilings, he has provided each room with its own particular character. The variety is fascinating: some ceilings are pitched, others saddle-backed or semimansarded, and still others completely different, depending for their shape on the complex play of the various roof styles of the house. The new volumes rise and descend almost at random, contributing to an unusual and fluid interpretation of interior space. Much of the charm of the house depends on such imaginative variations.

There is a consequent sense of openness in this summer retreat, a house created, the designer explains, "to take every advantage of the sun." Every effort has been made to bring light and air into the house. Even the gazebo has a large skylight.

But the problems of design extended well beyond the making of a summer house on the beach, since it is frequently used in the winter as well. In order to meet the demands of different seasons and different moods, effective combinations and compromises had to be found.

Overlooking the pool, for instance, is an enclosed solarium with a white tile floor and white-cushioned wicker furniture. Its summer freshness balances the sheltered living room, with its thickly upholstered sofas and leather chairs flanking a stainless-steel fireplace. Surfaces throughout the house run from smooth to reflective. But if the surfaces are cool, the reflections themselves are warm. The dominant white is offset by beiges, pale pinks and accents of royal blue—among many other colors.

"I had no particular theme in mind," says the designer. "There are just things around that I liked."

The "just things" in this case include a wide range of accessories—from a handsomely mounted wildebeest skull found in a shop on London's Pimlico Road to an ingenious array of mirrored skylights, reflecting on their many surfaces the brilliant light of Long Island.

A liberal use of lacquer, steel, plexiglass, tile and varnished rattan makes a crisp background for an assortment of natural curiosities with a seashore accent. Giant conch, nautilus and other exotic shells are displayed on Lucite stands. Here is a shell-encrusted box; there, a polished tortoise with brass head and feet. A tall sheaf of pampas grass in the living room echoes the old-fashioned Long Island beach house charm of the ancient wicker chairs in the trellised gazebo by the side of the pool. Pale durrie rugs soften the stark floor treatment, both in the living room and in the solarium.

A small greenhouse, open to the dining room, extends the flow of space and provides a suggestion of an outdoor atmosphere for the frequent dinner parties given in the house. Always interested in comfort and flexibility, the designer prefers several tables in the dining room rather than the impersonality of one large table.

"If you have four at a table for twenty," he says, "you lose something. The feeling really isn't intimate or comfortable anymore."

A collection of large semitropical plants adds a deep green to the many other colors found in the house. The plants, too, play an important role in that constant and carefully conceived interplay between the inside and the outside. The theme of tropical plants, in fact, carries into the swimming pool itself, which the designer has had painted with large palm frond motifs. At night they strike a delightful note of surprise as they flicker in the refractions of underwater lighting. The designer is quick to admit his fondness for palm trees. He even imported two large ones from Florida, at the beginning, to stand at either end of the poolside pavilion. Unhappily, they did not survive the Long Island winter and have been replaced with evergreens.

"They did give a marvelous look," says the designer sadly. "They were really handsome."

But Mr. de Santis is not one to dwell on the past. The palm trees are gone; the house now belongs to someone else. One design has been accomplished, and he looks forward to his next beach house. Will it be in the same genre?

"I don't think so," he says. "Perhaps the next one will be ultracontemporary."

Ultracontemporary, perhaps, but most surely not "stark, stark modern."

BELOW: *An aerial view reveals the Long Island bayfront residence that designer Michael de Santis transformed.* LOWER: *A Michael Ince sculpture dramatizes the main entrance.* LOWEST: *Sea shells and a polished tortoise with brass head and feet establish a seaside motif in the Living Room.* RIGHT: *Tile flooring, wicker and sailcloth contribute to the airiness of the Solarium.*

A wildebeest skull surveys the cool, crisp Dining Room. Though interior walls have been removed to admit more light and to create open spaces and large perspectives, twin polished-aluminum-and-glass tables encourage the kind of intimate dining Mr. de Santis favors. As in the adjacent solarium, white is the dominant color, offset by the natural tones of wicker and the pastel color accents introduced by a cantilevered buffet and the painting above it by Joseph Messina. The abstract painting over the living room sofa in the background is by Sanchez. A collection of semitropical plants reinforces the interplay between the interior and the exterior of the residence.

OPPOSITE: *A wooden deck surrounds the swimming pool and extends along the back of the updated Cape Cod structure. At the same level as the floor of the house, and of the same weathered gray as the shingles, it creates a smooth visual transition between interior and exterior. Alan West created the palm frond–inspired graphic treatment for the swimming pool; at night the frond motif seems to come alive, flickering in the myriad refractions of underwater lighting. The carefree waterside vacation complex includes, in addition to the beach house, a boat slip, tennis court, poolside dining pavilion and greenhouse.*

# TRANSLATING THE MEDITERRANEAN

Conceivably it could be a small Italian villa on the Amalfi coast. That the house is, in fact, situated in Beverly Hills merely increases its unusual charm. It is a warm and comfortable home that has mellowed over the years. There have been several different owners and, through a succession of improvements each has left a mark. Reed Springer is the most recent in that line of concerned and interested owners, and in the natural course of events he has introduced his own distinctive taste and personality in terms of remodeling and décor.

Designed by the architect Pierrepont Davis and built in 1939, the house is an expression of the Mediterranean idiom favored in the California of that era. It was planned to take every advantage of a small and steeply sloping site. So steep is the property, as a matter of fact, that the front door is some two stories below street level, and the bedrooms are on a lower level than the living and dining areas. Below them are a loggia and a terrace, and the vertical thrust from level to level contributes greatly to a unique appeal and an aura of quiet drama.

In addition, the house is a confirmation of the not surprising fact that an owner with imagination does not have to be a decorator or, indeed, use the services of one. Mr. Springer is not an interior designer by profession. He is, however, a collector of art and antiques, an enthusiastic student of design and—a lover of houses in general and of this multilevel one in particular.

"I didn't want it to look 'decorated' in any way," he says. "I simply wanted a pleasant setting for a rather haphazard and unpretentious collection of things I have gathered together over the years. But I suppose it's not quite as casual as it sounds. In retrospect, I did a great deal of work on the house, and I had a great deal of help."

Even though the house is small, he felt that a considerable amount of remodeling was necessary, and the work was executed by California architects John Woolf and Robert Koch. In the course of remodeling, some of the more intrusive aspects of the California/Mediterranean style were removed, and the additions that were made serve to underline and clarify the Italianate grace of the original design. For example, a remarkable staircase has been added, which curves upward around a large umbrella pine, a type of tree echoing the Italian cypresses found in the garden. To ascend the new staircase is to glimpse at each level a tantalizing portion of almost every room in the house. The effect is more than striking, and it succeeds in unifying and harmonizing setting and architecture in a seemingly effortless way.

This careful control of architecture, in terms of both space and detail, is one of the notable aspects of the original design as well as of the more recent additions that Reed Springer has inspired. Pierrepont Davis had a polished and exact feeling for proportions. In keeping with the design of the house, these proportions are classically Palladian. The additions made by John Woolf and Robert Koch carry forward the same theme and, as Mr. Springer points out, most of the rooms call for a chandelier, largely because of their square shapes and exact proportions. An alcove and fireplace were added to the master bedroom, and another entire bedroom was designed as well—part studio, filled with light and arranged on the principle of the double square, a favorite Palladian signature.

This combination of the original architectural design of 1939 and the additions supervised by Mr. Springer combine to give the house a rich European feeling and to create the impression that it is far older than it actually is. In large measure this sense results from the thick walls, the redwood ceiling in the living room, with its geometric patterns, and the small bistrolike dining room—all of which further a feeling of weathered foreign charm. It is difficult to remember that a large contemporary city surrounds this peaceful enclave on every side.

Mr. Springer's furniture, too, adds significantly to the European mood. He has collected what he carelessly calls a "hodgepodge" of French and Italian pieces. Some are Directoire, some Régence, but all are simple and uninvolved, country furnishings that are made mostly of fruitwood. He may speak somewhat casually of the pieces he has chosen, but they all reflect a very deliberate attitude and set of values. He has a distinct dislike for anything approaching the pretentious, and would far rather create a mood of quiet charm and comfort. It is for this reason that he delights in filling the house with plants and flowers, and in the proper season there are camellias from his own garden. He has also taken care to enhance the nighttime richness and drama of the house with pinpoint ceiling lighting. In fact, he is among the first to have used this type of lighting to accent objects other than paintings. Plants and statuary are lighted in this fashion, and the effect produced is mellow and uncommon.

To enter the house is to enter a special world, and Mr. Springer has placed much emphasis, not only on the interiors, but on the exterior architecture and the small garden, with its lovely flowers and cypresses. He retains the original terra-cotta color of the house, having quickly made the discovery that this color is accented by the setting sun in a particularly effective way. And the tall Italian cypresses add to the not unreasonable feeling that the house is actually hidden away in some romantic part of the Mediterranean coast.

"If I had to single out one particular aspect of the house that makes me personally find it so charming," says Mr. Springer, "I would without hesitation point to the multilevel construction. I think that's where the real magic lies."

Full of surprises and enchantments, the house today owes much to the work of professional designers. The architecture was striking from the beginning, and the additions were made with care and imagination. But the end result, the particular feeling characteristic of the house at the present time, has been largely the work of a nonprofessional—an owner in love with his house, willing to experiment and willing to maintain the integrity of the original design.

If there is a moral here—and surely there does not have to be one—it is that a professional interior designer is by no means always necessary to create a warm and inviting house. All that is required is taste and devotion and genuine interest. Reed Springer has these qualities in full measure.

"It is a house of continual discovery and change," he says. "I simply tried to take advantage of its basic charm and enhance it where I could."

An antique terra-cotta figure of Orpheus,
the poet and musician of Greek mythology,
sets a classical tone in the Living Room of
Mr. Reed Springer's multilevel hillside
residence in Beverly Hills. Italianate in
feeling and dominated by warm muted colors,
the elegantly proportioned room reflects the
Palladian influences that inspired architect
Pierrepont Davis when he designed the house
in 1939. The gentle curve of the Palladian
center window is echoed by the shape of the
ornate gilded overmantel trumeau and by
the rounded forms of Biedermeier tables,
hocked-leg stools and smaller ornamental
accessories. A graceful Louis XVI daybed
exemplifies the primarily 18th-century French
and Italian décor. A tiered tôle table and a
tôle lamp with painted shade contribute
subtle luster, while an Italian gilt and crystal
chandelier glistens overhead.

An impressive architectural detail—an elaborate redwood ceiling—adds warmth and geometric interest to the high-ceilinged Living Room. Four monochromatic antique overdoor paintings, mounted above the lavishly cushioned Louis XV sofa, reinforce the mellow tones that suffuse the room. The deliberately quiet milieu is accented by potted plants and vases of bright flowers.

BELOW: *A sunny alcove was added to the Master Bedroom when architects John Woolf and Robert Koch assisted Mr. Springer in remodeling the house. Faithful to the original Palladian concept, they introduced marbleized columns to soften the transition. Empire furnishings are enhanced by an Empire-patterned toile that upholsters the alcove and drapes the windows.*

OPPOSITE: *A vaulted ceiling heightens the drama and expanded perspective of the Dining Room, whose incontrovertible highlight is Los Angeles artist Douglas Riseborough's Venetian-inspired panoramic mural. Other touches of European-style exoticism include an Italian gilt chandelier, a circular gilt overdoor carving and a pair of parcel gilt columns flanking the French doors.*

OPPOSITE: *A light-filled Bedroom/Studio on a lower level, added during the remodeling, has the unusual advantage of a garden view on the same level as the windows. A skylight and an elaborate chandelier call attention to the high ceiling and the Palladian double-square principle of the room. Except for the Biedermeier bedside table, all the major furnishings are Italian.*

LEFT: *A view of the rear façade indicates the multilevel aspect of the structure, a trait that particularly pleases Mr. Springer. Highest are the living room and dining room, which adjoin the arch-framed balcony; canvas roller blinds silhouette the thin arches as well as shield the area. Protruding at left from the second level is the alcove of the master bedroom. On another level, poolside, is an intimate loggia; defined by columns and canvas draperies, it features a shell-shaped grotto settee and a carved-rope table. Despite the many changes he made, Mr. Springer chose to retain the original terra-cotta color of the house not only because it strengthens the romantic Mediterranean flavor but because it catches the light of sunset in an especially appealing manner.*

# A STATEMENT

# IN

# MODERN

A native of Louisville, Kentucky, interior designer Jay Spectre started his career in that city, specializing in period décor and importing antiques from Europe. But even then work in the traditional genre had begun to pall, and he found himself increasingly reluctant to design still another drawing room in the French manner. Happily, a move to New York City, where he started his own decorating firm, provided any number of new outlets for his creative energies. It allowed him, he feels, a fuller measure of personal expression and the opportunity of moving more positively in a contemporary direction.

A firm believer in different effects for different people, Mr. Spectre does not try to impose his own taste on those for whom he designs. He feels it is a mistake to carry anyone too far into unfamiliar territory and to attempt any change of personality through environment. Instead, he prefers to clarify the lifestyles of his clients.

"It's a wonderful thing to help people express themselves," he says. "It should never be a matter of duplicating someone else's taste."

When it came to designing the interiors of a house in Southampton for himself, as a retreat from the pressures of city life, he followed his own admonitions exactly. The result is a design that is totally personal. It stands as an effective summary of Jay Spectre's particular talents—a sense of purpose, an ability to decide quickly, an unwavering taste for the straightforward and a conviction that his intuitions are entirely reliable.

Everything seemed to fall into place when he first saw the property, in the Southampton woods on eastern Long Island. He knew instinctively that the time had come for him to build a house for himself, and he moved ahead with customary speed. Buying the land on the spot, without the confusions attendant on shopping around, he quickly told architect Harry Bates what he wanted in terms of space, exposures and materials.

Ground was broken within a week, and all the beauty of the site and its dense woodlands was respected and fully utilized. As it grew, the house became an organic part of the forest, rather than intruding upon it. A feeling for wood consequently informs the main structure, and the forest seems to flow in and out of the house itself. Large Ficus trees, palms and cut-leaf philodendrons flourish inside, along with giant begonias—separated from the outside only by what appears to be acres of tinted glass. In effect, the glass itself presents no greater barrier than the rays of light filtering through the trees. The total design of the classic modern house does not alter the site in any way; instead, it succeeds in making a subtle collaboration.

Interior secluded spaces—bedrooms, dressing rooms, bathrooms and kitchen—are glistening counterpoints to the voluminous and open living and dining areas. Here the natural profusion of the outdoors is shut out, and a logical human order prevails. The designer has used every modern technological device in a tour de force manipulation of stainless steel, mirrors, lighting and electronics. Discipline is rigid and, along with technological opulence and adroitness, there is the uncorrupted use of line and texture.

This integrity of materials is respected throughout. There are no tortured lines, no manipulated surfaces. Wood looks like wood, steel like steel, leather like leather and stone like stone. There is little feeling of coldness and rigidity, however, and an eclectic mix of art and accessories softens the overall effect. For example, a life-size Ernest Trova statue of *Falling Man* looks quite as much at home as the pair of sculptured African seats used as small tables in the living room.

There is an evident humanism and dignity in Mr. Spectre's house, a humanism embracing both past and present, both the primitive and the ultra-sophisticated. The major work of art dominating the living room—an immense, fourteen-foot Louise Nevelson wall piece executed specially for the room—sets the tone for the whole house with its sweeping rhythms and provocative counterpoints. Its simple sculptural elements are orchestrated into a masterwork of light and shadow, of surface tension and sculptural mass, of order and mystery.

There is no doubt that the designer's taste in art and objects runs to the extraordinary. In addition to the Nevelson and the Trova, there is a Jean Dubuffet

relief sculpture flanked by four Trova gouaches in the master bedroom. A brilliantly colored and luminous Vasarely statue stands on the dining room sideboard, and a large crystal vase by René Lalique, in the form of a coiled serpent, accents the massive low table in the living room. In the dining room there is a unique pair of rare black vases with a relief of lions by Davise, as well as an enormous K'ang Hsi vase filled with ferns.

The key word for this Southampton house is *sculptural*, whether in architecture, interior design or the selection of art and objects. It succeeds in maintaining a special integrity, since Jay Spectre himself designed all the furniture, with the exception of the chairs in the dining room. There is no decoration simply for the sake of decoration. There are few unnecessary objects and no paintings in the main rooms at all. Nothing is allowed to confuse or diminish the dramatic interplay and total effect of mass and volume and texture.

It is a direct house, a masculine house. Window treatments, for example, are handsome and plain, tinted glass taking the place of curtains or shades. There is little softness even in bedcovers and upholstery. Leather and suede appear throughout, often against *tête-de-nègre* backgrounds, and there are few rugs to break the flow of the slate flooring. Yet the result is neither cold nor severe, since the rich materials and the open volumes—along with the soft forest light filtering through the trees, and the luxuriant indoor planting—combine to give a feeling of warmth and comfort and harmony.

A broad spruce deck half surrounds the house and separates it from a bark-covered clearing. A pool, sunk into the deck and shaded by trees, has all the beauty of a natural pond. Once again, there is no intrusion on the setting. As the slate floors inside solidly anchor the architecture, so the plank decks outside blend with the surroundings. A logical order and harmony prevail.

In this first house created for himself, Jay Spectre has maintained the integrity of a unified statement. No doubt he will have other houses of his own in the future, but the Southampton design makes a difficult precedent to follow.

Designer Jay Spectre's country retreat at Southampton, Long Island has been described as "a space ship that landed in the woods." The T-shaped structure conceived by architects Harry Bates and Dale Booher in collaboration with Mr. Spectre seems to meld with its wooded environment. Sunlight glints on great expanses of window, and lush foliage casts deep shadows and reflections.

**OPPOSITE:** *Simplicity and consistency characterize the Living Room. Natural materials predominate, with flooring of slate, walls and ceiling of wood, and sofas of leather with suede cushions. The diminutive sculpture on the mantel is a Giacometti greyhound. Visible through the large overmantel window is a ship's smokestack that functions as a chimney.*

**BELOW:** *Dominating the Living Room and setting the tone for the total design is a monumental, 14-foot-high, wood construction by sculptor Louise Nevelson. In contrast to its undeviating geometry, decorative elements in the room evoke the animal kingdom: The Lalique vase on the massive low table is a coiled cobra and the African seats are stylized cats.*

*The plant-filled Dining Room—with three huge walls of solar bronze glass and six skylights of solar bronze plexiglass—has a greenhouse atmosphere. Mr. Spectre designed the dining table and sideboard, both of which are fabricated of materials found throughout the house: stainless steel and slate. Resting on the sideboard is a construction by Victor Vasarely.*

LEFT AND BELOW LEFT: *Two views of the Guest Room reveal the many traits it shares with the rest of the residence: Except for the suede cloth-upholstered wall behind the bed, all of the walls are wood paneled; again, the floor is dark slate; and the furniture is brushed stainless steel covered in leather. Two French chairs and a small African rug are cosmopolitan contributions. The bedside table swivels to serve as a tray and contains a multiplicity of electrical controls.*
RIGHT: *A wall of solar bronze mirror reflects the Master Bedroom, with its channeled leather-upholstered bed and chocolate brown walls, ceiling and carpeting. Above the bed is a Jean Dubuffet sculpture and to the sides are collages by Ernest Trova. Recessed in the mirrored wall is a stainless-steel cabinet with a tambour door that conceals a large television screen.*

# AN ESTATE
# IN THE
# DUTCH COLONIAL
# MANNER

"When I was confronted with the problem of doing this great house over," says Jack Warner, "I came to the conclusion that it would be both boring and expensive to arrange it in the traditional manner."

The California architect is talking about his favorite house in the whole world—his own. *Constantia* has been one of the jewels of Santa Barbara architecture since 1930, even though it is a unique departure from the almost obligatory stuccoed and red-tiled Hispanic look of most Montecito dwellings. Constantia was built for Arthur Meeker, an executive of the Armour Company of Chicago, by Ambrose Cramer, one of that era's many gifted and imaginative architects. A Beaux-Arts graduate and a protégé of the renowned David Adler, Cramer specialized in extravagant houses and was determined to make a masterpiece for the Meekers—who happened to be his in-laws.

Creating a unique home in that decade in Montecito, which already contained some of the most impressive architecture in the United States, was not easy. But Cramer did it, and he did it with great élan. He decided that he would design Constantia in the style of the Dutch architecture of Cape Town, South Africa. And it is said that he was inspired by one of Cecil Rhodes's houses, which was called by the same name.

When Jack Warner first saw the house he fell completely in love with it. "And I lusted after it for thirteen years," he says. Patience was rewarded, however, and Mr. Warner, of the architectural firm of Warner and Gray, in Montecito, did eventually acquire the house. But, once he had it, he was not entirely sure how to handle the problem of interior decoration. He did, on the other hand, know that he wanted to do all the interiors himself.

"I've worked with top decorators all over the country," he says, "and I admire their work enormously. But every once in a while I like to do the interiors myself. It makes for a totally unified result, I think, and I was willing to take chances. Chances I couldn't take, for example, with the Birnam Wood Golf Club down the road from Constantia, where we had to be more traditional and conservative. Although I've never studied interior decorating as such, the basic design courses I took at the University of Southern California were relevant to all interior work, as well as to architecture. Nevertheless, I attacked the problem of Constantia with some trepidation, plus a lot of love and enthusiasm."

The first thing to do, he realized, was to dispense with the venetian blinds and heavy draperies that covered the windows and made the interiors so dark. Eliminating these revealed the lovely windows themselves, windows that emerged almost as sculpture, with their fine detail and filigree work. To preserve this quality, he left the windows uncovered.

Next came the color of the walls. The existing magenta, raspberry, green and gold were not exactly the colors he had in mind. By painting all the interiors white—with the exception of natural oak beams and other woodwork—he gave unity to the house and allowed himself the freedom to select the décor in just about any style he chose. His basic tastes were simple, however, and he was content to use natural materials and textures, along with a few more traditional furnishings.

Typical of his furniture is the living room table, with a travertine top and supported by a huge stump with the bark still on it. In the window recesses there are now four immense Chinese wine jars, made around 1850, resting on sections of Santa Barbara palms. Near the fireplace are large capitals from columns the architect collected in Spain, Italy and Mexico. They make remarkably convenient tables. And the primitive wooden chairs are the remnants of some seven hundred he bought inexpensively when the Del Mar Race Track management decided they were not contemporary enough.

Above the fireplace is a white water-buffalo skull with black horns, which recalls the original South African inspiration for the house. Here and there are outsized seashells and large turtle shells on the walls. The tiles around the fireplace in the smoking room are said to have been produced after studies by the artist Goya. None of these effects, however, seem out of keeping with the contemporary sculpture Mr. Warner has collected, such as Bruce and Clonard Thomas's seven-foot-tall *Firefall*, made of red polyester resin or Bruce Thomas's flowing

sculpture entitled *Pearlescent*.

One of the most intriguing details of all is a favorite with the architect's three children: their "secret door," which leads to a downstairs room. They push the tile wall on its right side, and the hidden door swings open magically to admit them to a most mysterious realm, the downstairs powder room.

On the outside the U-shaped house reproduces Cape Town architecture most accurately. There are six flamboyant gables, each with a graceful scroll pattern. Derived from the Late Medieval Italian churches where façades were added to conceal the nave, they successfully hide the peaked second-story roof, a feature of the house that would not be particularly attractive in an unadorned state.

The driveway leading to the house is memorable, beginning at the great stone pillars of the entrance and winding past the guest house—a charming miniature, in itself an architectural preview of the main building. There are at least fifty macadamia trees on the grounds, and through them glimpses of the Pacific Ocean, only a few miles away, can be seen. For the house is situated in a unique location on one of the rare hills in Montecito that affords a view of both sea and mountains. The 75-by-150-foot pool reflects the hills as well as the formal planting and the mirrored image of a classic and timeless house. Swimming peacefully in a watery world of her own is Gladys, the pet duck who quacks contentedly. She seems to be saying that all is well at Constantia.

The lure of Santa Barbara is very great. The Spaniards, who first settled here, called it *La Tierra Adorada*, "The Beloved Land," and the reasons for their appreciation are clearly evident today. The city lies peacefully on a sheltered plain—on one side, a wide beach and the Pacific Ocean; on the other, the magnificent backdrop of the Santa Ynez Mountains.

Little has changed since 1895, when Frank Sands wrote in his book *Santa Barbara at a Glance*: "It is too beautiful to be marred . . . it seems well to leave here and there an oasis of beauty, where man can flee from the rattle of the dollar, where his better nature can assert itself, where his eyes can behold the beauty of earth, air and sea."

OPPOSITE: *The architectural style of* Constantia, *described as Dutch-South African, was adapted from the Cape Town residence of Sir Cecil Rhodes. Before the main house is a 75-by-150-foot pool, and surrounding it are thickset camphor trees and black acacia hedges. The four-acre estate, located in the heart of Montecito, has been a Santa Barbara landmark since its construction in 1930.*

ABOVE: *Upon acquiring the unique residence, architect Jack Warner updated it inside and out, choosing to design the interiors himself. His interest in modern art is apparent throughout the 14-room house and in the garden. On the lawn near the oceanside façade, the polyester-resin sculpture* Geminescence, *by Bruce Thomas, adds a bright dash of color and challenges the traditional setting.*

LEFT: *Large-scale casual appointments and natural materials in the Living Room contrast with the formal exterior. Chinese dragon jars on Santa Barbara palm-stump pedestals and an outsized turtle shell above a Moroccan bone-inlaid cabinet complement log furniture upholstered in thick Portuguese carpeting. Sculptures are by Bruce and Clonard Thomas.*

ABOVE: *Another view of the sunlit Living Room points up a row of typically Dutch small-mullioned windows, the oak-plank floor and oak ceiling beams. An absence of draperies lets in the light and calls attention to the interesting architecture; white paint throughout unifies the design. The travertine tabletop, supported by a pine stump with the bark still intact, is surrounded by canvas-cushioned hickory chairs.*

*Afternoon sun and a blazing fire cast a warm glow on the walnut-paneled Smoking Room. Period furnishings include a French daybed and a Chinese Chippendale chair. The fireplace is decorated with tiles painted after studies by the artist Goya; above them is a drawing by Richards Ruben. Bruce Thomas's silver sculpture Serendipity enhances the draped table.*

Natural light admitted freely through undraped
windows completes the color scheme of the Guest
Room—resplendent in white. A Chinese Chippendale
mirror graces the wall above a fireplace outlined
in 18th-century Delft tiles. Bruce Thomas's
polyester-resin sculpture Pearlescent and a palm-
stump table supporting an 18th-century Chinese
daffodil-filled cachepot add aesthetic appeal.

# A
# WORLD TRAVELER'S
# COSMOPOLITAN
# COMFORT

The house is only fifteen minutes away from the busy and contemporary city of Dallas, Texas. It might, however, be in another country and in another time. For its surroundings are mellow and comfortably rural, with aged oaks spreading their gnarled branches across the narrow road, and arches of green everywhere. Squirrels dart from hedges and disappear over great expanses of green grass, the quiet broken only by the chattering of birds. Foliage is abundant, the various shades of green changing from light to dark in the slanting rays of the afternoon sun. Not far away is Turtle Creek, one of two streets that Frank Lloyd Wright called "the most beautiful in the world."

For importer Robert Floyd, of Fitz & Floyd, the whole area is a sort of paradise. He himself spends five months a year traveling in Europe and the Orient, where he is occupied gathering dinnerware and giftware for his company. But his thoughts are never far from Texas. As he says, "My idea of a pleasant time is staying right here."

"Here," to Mr. Floyd, is a Georgian-style house that radiates quiet charm, both inside and outside. Like the area in which it is located, the house has a pleasant feeling of being tucked away. And, in fact, it is—although only fifteen minutes away—far from the slick skyscrapers and air-conditioned malls and concrete highways of modern Texas.

"I had admired this house for many years," says Mr. Floyd. "Then one day it was suddenly for sale. I walked right in and bought it!"

Of the three residences that California-based interior designer Jack Lowrance has decorated for him, this is by far the most formal and traditional.

"I'm not at all sure that taste is a blessing," says Robert Floyd. "The more I grow and develop, the more dissatisfied I seem to be with what I have, and the more eager I am for intrinsically better pieces. For example, take those statues in the entrance hall. They are among the earliest illustrations of the use of glass for eyes in wooden sculpture, a technique unknown before the sixteenth century. My statues are of some of the disciples of Buddha, and the Orientals used them for prayer. Well, in 1964 the temple that housed them was torn down to make a section of highway for the Olympic Games. I was asked if I wanted them, and fortunately my level of taste was far enough along that I could appreciate them. The curator at the San Francisco Museum tells me that I have an exceptional collection of these figures. And I have them today, because I was at the right place at the right time—the right time in terms of my own cultural development."

So it was important to Mr. Floyd that the interiors for the house he recently acquired in Dallas express in some degree the new levels of appreciation and self-awareness he had reached. To achieve this he sought the help of Jack Lowrance, a fellow Texan who quickly understood the fine nuances Mr. Floyd was seeking.

The result is that the new décor of each room is presented with understatement and an attention to detail. Understatement, in fact, is perhaps the most notable characteristic of the house, a characteristic creating a special quality of authoritative calm. There is nothing in an individual room that commands immediate attention or distracts from the totality, but there is a rich accumulation of detail. Possibly, like good paintings, good interiors require a certain amount of time before their virtues are fully understood and enjoyed.

Jack Lowrance, quite in keeping with Mr. Floyd's wishes, thinks of design in terms of the uniqueness of the individual. Above all, he does not believe in using theatrical effects.

"I don't think people like being in a setting they feel they have to live up to," says the designer. "They prefer an environment that simply allows them to be themselves, a place where nothing out of the ordinary is expected of them."

In a profession that is occasionally ostentatious, Mr. Lowrance still retains—and surely Mr. Floyd appreciated this quality—the country directness of west Texas where he was born. His is a disarmingly modest approach.

"I never try to impose my own ideas," he says.

It is not an original point, but it is a valid one. An interior designer is paid for a degree of expertise. In what does that expertise consist? Many people have good taste, a sense of color and the ability to select and arrange their fabrics and furniture—Mr. Floyd definitely has these qualities—and the results may be enchanting. The professional designer will have another ability and in a way it can be a more important one: He will be able to give his clients, not always what they think they want, but what they really should have. It is no secret that the nonprofessional is often too close to see things with the proper clarity or perspective.

Thus, Mr. Floyd and the designer were able to collaborate on the Dallas project to the best possible advantage. As a collector and a traveler, Mr. Floyd was able to give the interior designer a wealth of material: fine Ming, T'ang and Edo porcelains, a variety of Louis XV furniture, a Fu dog from Japan—among much else. The problem then became how to harmonize these elements of the past in a way at once traditional and contemporary. The resulting décor honors the past—and yet is clearly in keeping with the contemporary world.

Like any interior designer of merit, Mr. Lowrance was able to understand instinctively the direction in which the owner wished the décor to go. Understatement was to be the key to the design, and the rich heritage of the past was to be honored. Comfort was of no small significance, and the resulting interiors would reflect—as, indeed, they should—the personality and interests of the owner.

"I appreciate contemporary furniture," says Mr. Floyd, "because I like big, overstuffed comfort. But I find that something entirely contemporary is apt to be cold and sterile. I need warmth, and I need those beautiful reminders of man's heritage. I suppose that's why I have been such an enthusiastic collector over the years, and no doubt it's why I'm in the business I am in. I think I have the taste and education for selecting individual items—antiques, that sort of thing. But I certainly needed a designer to pull everything together.

"This house is very comfortable for me now, very fulfilling. I'm grateful for it, even though my business keeps me away a good deal of the time."

Robert Floyd leans back onto a sofa, as if savoring each moment he has in his home—before he will have to leave on his travels once again.

LEFT: *A collection of Japanese carved-wood* Rakan—*figures representing the disciples of Buddha—creates a spiritual ambience in the Entrance Hall of the Robert Floyd residence in Dallas. Among the earliest examples of wooden sculptures with glass eyes, these late Muromachi Period figures cluster about an antique Italian mirror and console.*
OPPOSITE: *The Oriental influence gently pervades a corner of the Living Room where a 16th-century Japanese bodhisattva sits in lotus position between a pair of Ming Dynasty jars. A collection of ivory netsuke, a 17th-century Japanese screen above a velvet-upholstered and tasseled love seat, and Chinese silk-embroidered pillows perpetuate the distinctive Far Eastern flavor.*

RIGHT: *A crystal chandelier sparkles in the Dining Room, while a bronze deer from Thailand placidly surveys the scene from its perch in front of a Vasica painting.*
BELOW: *A more ferocious onlooker is the expressively carved 17th-century Japanese wood Fu dog. The Dining Room table itself is inhabited by a collection of porcelains from the Orient—small male figures who serve as ashtrays and a delicate Japanese female dancer. The centerpiece, a lacquered container filled with spiky proteas, echoes the floral motif of the fabric chosen for draperies and chair upholstery.*

LEFT: *A graceful pair of 18th-century Venetian footstools nestle invitingly before the Living Room fireplace. Illuminating the mantel are two Louis XV crystal girandoles; between the fixtures an Oriental porcelain figure rides a deer.*

253

LEFT: *A collection of Chinese and Japanese porcelain objects prompted the decision to define the Sitting Room in blue and white. Designer Jack Lowrance chose a leafy chinoiserie-inspired print for the comfortable sofa and chairs as well as for the valance and draperies. Batik pillows extend the blue-and-white theme and introduce a geometric counterpoint. Japanese lacquered tables resting on the terrazzo floor provide still another dark-to-light contrast characteristic of this airy room.*

ABOVE: *An antique Chinese needlework image of birds typifies the muted harmony of the restful Master Bedroom. Classically situated upon the Louis XVI mantel are two Napoleon III marble spheres; the intricately carved and inlaid mirror is 17th-century English.*

# OASIS

# IN

# PALM SPRINGS

The pine-covered San Jacinto Mountains rise dramatically in the background, and the multicolored desert stretches out to the east. All the pleasures of Palm Springs lie conveniently at hand: the tennis and the golf; the swimming and the horseback riding; the sun and the crystal air. The California resort grows more popular yearly, and increasingly people from all parts of the country—and the world—have made it their winter home.

Other fortunate people, like interior designer Stephen Chase, have elected to have year-round residences in this desert oasis. He has created a contemporary house, secluded behind the aged walls of a former estate. The privacy of the spot is delightful, the atmosphere international. For the house could just as well be in Morocco or on a Greek island, instead of being merely two hours from the metropolis of Los Angeles, where Mr. Chase also keeps a small apartment.

But his home is essentially in Palm Springs, and he feels with some justification that he now has the perfect house in the perfect setting. But it is a characteristic of designers that they are never entirely satisfied with their work. As Mr. Chase says, "I know I could redo the house today and make a good many improvements."

It is difficult to imagine what they might be, since what he has already created contains innumerable refinements and has achieved a high level of finish. Everything was planned with clarity and precision. There are no accidents or bursts of carefree spontaneity. This is a house of deliberation, and every inch of it has been conscientiously considered. Textures are balanced one against the other. Matte-finish metal reflects against polished steel, and soft and hard edges combine in counterpoint. Natural light, filtering through in various degrees of intensity, emphasizes this interplay of surfaces, and the atmosphere is quite in harmony with the beauty of the desert setting itself.

Pure design is the focus, and it is somewhat severe in its exactness. There are few antiques in the house, and Mr. Chase's collections have been chosen for decorative and personal reasons—and for their intrinsic charm as well.

"There's nothing of any great value here," he says. "If need be, it could all be replaced. Being a decorator spoils you in one respect, I think. For if I had antiques, I would want the finest. Not only can't I afford them, but there aren't that many available anymore. And I think I would feel a tremendous responsibility I don't want to have. But I do like to borrow from the nature of antiques. I try to duplicate the quality of fine antique furniture, for example, by finding the very best craftsmen that I can and by having them use the best materials. Quality is an overworked word, I know, but that is really what I like to add to contemporary design.

"I still think people want the luxury of what used to be called 'living in the grand manner.' And the same luxury is available today. It simply must be interpreted in contemporary terms. I feel exactly the same way about painting and sculpture, and I admire new artists precisely because their work reflects the present moment.

"And certainly my own thinking changes constantly. A few years ago, for example, I dismissed mirrors as simply a contrivance in decorating. Today, however, I use them as a means of replacing lost space. And the use of mirrors enables me to make a 4,000-square-foot home look as if it were 8,000. It all comes down to a matter of practicality, I suppose. There are many limitations in modern life."

For this reason his house in Palm Springs is so carefully arranged that he can entertain fifty guests for the evening and have nothing to do next morning but empty the ashtrays. The very absence of coasters for glasses is indicative of his attitude.

"I don't like little safety things," he says. "In this house you can come in from the swimming pool wearing a wet bathing suit, and not hurt a thing. I don't think preciousness belongs in today's living. But that doesn't mean that I believe in the sterile look, which is often erroneously thought of as contemporary. I think that sort of look is negative decorating, and I don't think human feelings can be reduced to cold floors and pillowed furniture, or stamped out with wicker and tree-trunk tables. I wouldn't design a room that diminishes people. That's certainly not the point of interior design."

On the contrary, he designs rooms that show people to their advantage, rooms that make people their most comfortable. In this respect Mr. Chase's approach is consistent—whether he is designing a Colonial mansion in Seattle or a contemporary house in Hawaii or a traditional apartment in New York City. Whatever the style or genre of a particular project, however, he insists on making it relevant to the present moment. For example, sometimes he arranges traditional furniture in a new way or quite often he creates his own custom-designed pieces.

Design, in his view, is essentially a matter of thinking in new terms, and of finding solutions that harmonize with contemporary life. In his own house there are innumerable clever solutions, such as using commercial tile to cover the bar, or placing electrical outlets in bathroom drawers for shavers, hair driers and so forth.

"A beautiful house that doesn't work," he says, "is something like the child who fantasizes about living in a castle. Fine, but he'll *still* have the problem of brushing his teeth and combing his hair. I want to simplify these things as much as I can, to make everything as convenient as possible."

His search for simplification and convenience has required a good deal of careful editing. He has tried to eliminate all excess and use only what is necessary for comfort and convenience.

"There is little here that distracts me," he comments. "My apartment in Beverly Hills, on the other hand, does seem to be cluttered with a good deal of memorabilia, with things I've had for years and can't bear to part with. But I only use the apartment when I come to town for business. It's full of things, I admit, but at least the apartment is all beige. The color isn't overwhelming."

Not that Mr. Chase has anything against overwhelming colors. Among his current projects, for example, is a house with an emerald green floor and a bold use of primary colors on the exterior. These colors, dramatic as they may be, will be presented with all the thoroughness and painstaking attention to detail given to his own monochromatic house in Palm Springs. For Stephen Chase is a professional and a most logical interior designer.

BELOW: *Massive copper-clad doors mark the entrance to designer Stephen Chase's Palm Springs residence.* LOWER LEFT: *Soaring architectural vitrines give the Living Room a dramatic vertical thrust. Furnishings, plants and objets d'art are grouped on a cool expanse of travertine.* LOWER RIGHT: *A mirrored ceiling extends the intimate loft above the living room.*

An antique Pekinese dog house, an indoor tree
and a sand-textured stairway wall with a
niche housing a Japanese wooden figure preface a
view of the living room's sunken Conversation
Area, directly below the loft. The multilevel flow of
space and subtle interplay of textures and
surfaces are precisely defined; plants trailing over
balcony walls soften the edges of the architecture.

RIGHT: *Sunlight passes through tall sliding doors to a section of the Living Room adjacent to the terrace. An African alligator carving and a painting by Stephen Harger accent the neutral-toned environment. Palms reach upward, merging the exterior landscape with the interior space.*
BELOW: *Mr. Chase used commercial tiles to cover the Bar Area of the living room. Visible from the inviting upholstered bar chairs is a terrace view dramatically extended by a mirrored wall beyond the swimming pool.*

Richard Kishady's exotic jungle mural and a number of vigorous plants provide a basis for the Dining Room's naturalistic atmosphere. A giant gnarled tree trunk supports the glass-topped dining table with its cactus-filled centerpiece and set of upholstered bamboo chairs. The solidity of another wall has been opened up to effectively display sculptures, shells, baskets and pottery.

OPPOSITE: *Careful attention to the texture of every surface is exemplified in the Master Bedroom. Raw silk covers the walls and chiseled beams section the reed-paneled ceiling. The geometric pattern of the rug is similarly repeated on the bedcovering. A pair of Louis XV–style chairs attend a contemporary desk. A Duane Wakeman landscape provides quiet artistry.*

ABOVE: *The Powder Room's tortoiseshell–patent leather walls shimmer between brass strips. A pair of Chinese cloisonné vases and a Chinese gold-leafed woodcarving are reflected by the mirrored wall above the marble sink counter.* RIGHT: *The Master Bathroom's sunken tub, custom fixtures and sleek, efficient blinds are in keeping with the severe yet luxurious logic that characterizes the total design. A Moroccan chair, a 14th-century Cambodian stone torso and a painting by Marilyn Lowe add finishing touches.*

# THE
# HOUSE OF
# FOUR
# FOUNTAINS

"You drift from something minor—a way to pass your time, with one assistant to help—and eventually it becomes really something."

Mrs. Archibald Brown's summing up of her more than fifty years as a New York interior designer, the founder and still active head of McMillen, Inc., is characteristically simple and succinct. But it does need a gloss. Mrs. Brown works and moves with unhurried grace, but she does not actually "drift," either physically or metaphorically. And "really something" should be interpreted as comprehending not only McMillen's enduring ability to keep abreast of change for over half a century, but also its capacity to do so without abandoning its founder's standards: respect for tradition, devotion to quality, excellence of workmanship, and a concern for the probity of taste.

To Mrs. Brown, in her eighties, interior designing is by now second nature. Her fellow designer and admirer Billy Baldwin says, "She considers decoration, not as an end in itself, but as part of a way of life." Anyone who knows her understands that she is by nature as disinclined to dictate about decorating as about living. But her experience and reputation are such that she is often consulted as an oracle and—if only in self-defense—she is prepared to mention some of the principles that have guided her throughout her long career.

"I try to design rooms around their architecture," she says, "or to create architecture for rooms where none exists. Rooms should reflect the personality of their owner. Best for a decorator to resist the temptation of producing a pretentious or novel effect. Pretension palls, fads fade."

The charming house on East Fifty-fifth Street in New York City, where Mrs. Brown, then Mrs. Drury McMillen, lived when she founded the firm in 1924, is still her working headquarters. It is supplemented by considerable office space in a modern building across the street. But for years she has lived in another apartment. In former house and present apartment, interiors bear the gentle but perceptible imprint of the personality of the designer.

Perhaps, however, it is her country house at Southampton that provides the most telling example of her architectural and decorative approach. *Four Fountains* was originally designed and built for a client in 1930 by her second husband, the late Archibald M. Brown, a well-known architect. The client was rather unusual in wanting a dilettante's pleasure dome near the ocean, not a conventional seaside house. In addition, he required a special hall where he could entertain his friends with amateur theatricals and concerts and films.

In 1942, when World War II was on and amateur theatricals were off, the property with its nineteen acres of land came on the market. Mr. and Mrs. Brown decided to buy it and convert the pleasure dome into their summer residence.

It was a daring decision for the period. The extravaganza of the 1930s had turned into a 1940s white elephant. Its conversion entailed the transformation of a vast interior area—the former auditorium, forty feet long and wide and twenty feet high—into a habitable living room, with the addition of windows and a fireplace. It also required the substitution of two double bedrooms with bathrooms for what had once been a raised stage, and the removal of a large church organ. A year's hard work by Mr. and Mrs. Brown saw the reconstruction and decoration through to a successful conclusion.

"It was an extraordinary achievement," says Billy Baldwin. "Miles ahead of its time in concept."

In its present reincarnation Four Fountains is one of the most attractive of Southampton's private houses. True, the original acreage has been considerably reduced through gifts of land to the younger generation, and the neighboring sands that once stretched pristine and untrodden at the end of a country lane have become part of a much-frequented public beach. But even now the stoutly built stone buildings, with a circular courtyard of flagstone lined with superb English boxwood, and the front and back doors of the main house, framed with pairs of cryptomeria, seem ensconced in an immaculate and indestructible world of their own.

Within the house a small but pleasantly formal entrance hall, its walls and floor of crab-orchard stone, leads into the living room. It is the former auditorium, and all memories of its original stark-

ness have been effectively banished by pastel walls and deft groupings of furniture. These groupings minimize the enormous proportions of the room and divide it into a number of distinct but related living areas. Comfortable sofas and a variety of conveniently placed chairs invite and encourage conversation. A library/dining area offers a setting for meals at small round tables by a window overlooking the garden. There is also a bar and a music corner that round out the functions of this room.

"Functional intimacy" is how another old friend and frequent houseguest, the artist and designer Van Day Truex, describes the unique quality of Four Fountains. He adds—and it is no mean compliment from one who is a knowledgeable and inspiring critic of interiors—that Eleanor Brown's treatment of her Southhampton living room, in particular, is "the very best handling of all-purpose space that I know about."

Throughout the house the furniture is predominantly eighteenth-century French and Italian. Fabric colors are mild by current standards, but agreeably unemphatic and easy on the eye, never precious or weak. According to Mrs. Brown, the furniture "was just an accumulation of the things we had collected together.

"We bought very little," she says. "In the thirty-odd years that I have lived here I have only recovered the sofas and chairs once—and in the same colors as before. But the majority of my friends, even the young ones, seem to think that the place is more or less all right."

Her reference to the approval of the young is revealing as well as endearing. At McMillen, where work is increasingly concerned with projects for contemporary apartments, offices, banks and commerical houses—from the United States to the Middle Eastern countries—much of the designing is confidently entrusted to the younger members of the staff. The results have always been happy ones. Understanding breeds understanding, and confidence inspires confidence. It is the way in which Mrs. Brown has always worked. And it is not necessary to be an octogenarian to know that good plants grow from good roots.

*To unify the palazzo-scaled Living Room—forty feet square with a twenty-foot-high ceiling—Mrs. Brown followed a classic tradition. She created a central axis with a graceful translucent chandelier and, directly below it, an 18th-century Italian table resting on a bold-patterned rug. She then divided the periphery of the vast space into intimate conversation groups.*

RIGHT: *Doyenne interior designer Eleanor Brown stands at the entrance of the Main House at* Four Fountains, *her country home located at Southampton, Long Island. Built in 1930 by the designer's architect husband, the late Archibald M. Brown, the residence features a circular flagstone driveway lined with English boxwood and a pair of cryptomeria fringing the front door.* BELOW RIGHT: *Mr. Brown chose the same mottled crab-orchard stone for the gabled roof and for the walls and floor of the small formal Entrance Hall.*

RIGHT AND BELOW: *A smooth transition between Living Room conversation areas was achieved by the use of a long Italian Empire fruitwood table, flanked by a pair of Louis XV armchairs, centered in front of one of the long walls. Its warm and lustrous surface serves as a mini-gallery suitable for displaying works of art.*

The fireplace, added in the 1940s when the Living Room was transformed from an auditorium, provides the focal point for a major seating arrangement. Prominently exhibited upon the marble mantel is Wheeler William's sculpture Figure of Summer. Tall windows, framed by fringed draperies, call attention to the high ceiling and graceful moldings.

OPPOSITE: *The muted tonalities of Raoul Dufy's painted toile hanging of circus horses and trainers harmonize with the carefully controlled color scheme of the Living Room, which is also characterized by an Italianate simplicity. Although ample in size, the sofa and Louis XV chairs are nevertheless gracefully proportioned and well scaled to the dimensions of the large room.*

ABOVE: *The spacious living room includes a Dining Area graced with a peaceful view of the verdant landscape. Italian Directoire chairs, part of a set of ten, surround a small draped table set with Queensware.* ABOVE RIGHT: *When the house was reconstructed, the stage that had been used originally for amateur theatricals was enclosed and converted into this Bedroom and another one. The velvet-covered antique bed is Spanish; the console beneath the curtained windows is 18th-century Italian.*

# AN ARTIST'S BEACHSIDE EXOTICA

Jack Baker lives in what looks like a Jack Baker painting, by the side of the sea, some thirteen miles south of Santa Barbara, California. Actually his house, once a private garage, stands on an acre of ground in the midst of a ferocious confusion and glorious and exotic tangle of garden, several hundred feet from the ocean.

If you happen to call on the artist, make it in the afternoon, since he paints unfailingly from five in the morning until two in the afternoon. You will probably find him feasting his eyes on a floral smorgasbord: bougainvillaea, hibiscus, plumeria, datura, jasmine, fuchsia and fifteen varieties of ginger, all blending luxuriantly with tree ferns, Ficus, philodendron and assorted fruit trees. If it sounds like a jungle, it is—but an organized one, composed with care and studied carelessness, with a constant eye for color and symmetry.

He extends a hand as he walks toward you. "You see, I'm basically a grower, a farmer," says Mr. Baker, gesturing animatedly at the Rousseau-like forest around him.

He is dressed in an unbuttoned shirt with the tail out, safari pants and patent leather pumps. Since he uses his shirt for a paint rag, he is a walking palette of all the Baker colors that have become his trademark and that are increasingly imitated: geranium crimson, cinnabar yellow, alizarin crimson, manganese and cerulean blue and sap green.

The artist is a bright-eyed, wiry, ageless Puck of a man with a tousled head of dark hair. He puts down the machete, with which he has been hacking off acanthus leaves. "Everything grows so fantastically here," he says, "that you really need a flamethrower in order to hold your own against the plants. Just look at that oleander!"

He leads the way to the patio, past Italian wine baskets full of seashells he has recently collected. The patio is a roofless affair Mr. Baker designed as he went along, the way the entire house was remodeled. Here he has colonial columns that do not go with the Siamese pagoda or the Balinese fish on top of the pagoda or the eight trompe l'oeil zebra skins on the inner walk—and these do not go with anything in the rest of the house, either.

An understanding friend, interior designer Dennis Peterson, helped with the mélange, and somehow all the theoretically incompatible elements work, as in an expertly blended clam-fish-chicken-sausage paella. There are tall flowering banana trees, palms and staghorn ferns at the side of the house. One could be in the middle of Zamboanga or even in Basilan.

A half-finished canvas is on an easel in the middle of the courtyard. It is of some plants, fuchsia and plumeria, as seen through a window framed by louvered shutters. The plants are real, the models in pots in front of him, while the louvered shutters are from memory. He has painted so many louvered windows and gazebos and pergolas that he needs no props. But he always derives fresh inspiration from having living plants "pose" for him.

"I always work from life," he explains.

In the long main room of the house the first thing to greet the eye is an exotic animal skull on a Greek amphora, then a sheaf of wheat tied with a red ribbon, then a giant spider crab looking alive at the feet of two Indian temple figures on a refectory table. Then there are nests—dozens of bird nests, from hummingbirds to wild pigeons—placed on shelves near the kitchen.

"Dad's on a nest kick," says a pretty girl with the hint of an English accent. Liza, on a visit from London, is sitting on the floor, painting a canvas.

"Isn't that great?" says her father, looking over her shoulder and patting her. "And her sister India is becoming a good painter, too."

Mr. Baker loves to teach—especially the young. He hated to give up instructing at the Santa Barbara high school after ten years, but teaching was making too many demands on his time.

"As it is," he explains, "right now, I'm six commissions behind." And he gestures at four big unfinished canvases around the room.

In the afternoon, with the equivalent of a full day's work already behind him, Jack Baker heads for the beach and the fabled Rincon surf. Or he may spend the time adding to his collection of hundreds of shells, for some as yet undetermined project. Such enthusiasm and zest are the qualities that attract people to him and lead collectors to his paintings. In the past years his work seems to have caught on enormously. He recently completed some mural commissions in New York and has had exhibitions in the Midwest, Texas, San Francisco, Palm Springs and London.

"I want whatever I do to have vitality," he says. "I'm not satisfied with mediocrity or the commonplace. I like the exotic and strikingly unusual."

His love of the exotic can be seen in almost all of the artifacts around the big living room: the tall Balinese umbrellas, the Indian temple toys, the wooden horses on wheels, the brace of large black elephants fit for a young rajah—all souvenirs of his travels around the world.

"I was born in Texas," he says, "and came to California at a young age. Then I studied painting at the *Académie Julian* in Paris. Didn't everybody? Since then I've lived all over India and Africa. In Ethiopia I worked for the emperor for three years. When he hired me, he was under the misguided impression that I could teach mechanical drawing. This came as quite a shock to both of us! I loved the country, but after a while I was ready to move on."

He is not anxious to discuss his theories of painting at any great length. "Ingres said that drawing is the touchstone of art, that an artist can learn all there is to know about color in an afternoon. But I keep learning new things, discovering new colors and combinations. I think I'm painting better than I have ever done before. But I'm just going my own way, doing whatever satisfies me. To hell with the mainstream. I don't even know what the mainstream is—I'm too busy painting my own statement seven days a week."

But he always has time for fun, to give a periodic party or celebration. In fact, there is one tonight. There will be a few writers, a few socialites, a few artists, most of them Santa Barbarans. But there are a couple of hours before the guests are due to arrive. So the artist pours a drink in a large glass, picks up a brush and begins to attack a ten-foot canvas with a great gob of fuchsia paint.

"I like everything to be larger than life," says Jack Baker. "Especially life!"

The design of artist Jack Baker's house, a converted private garage located a few hundred yards from the Pacific near Santa Barbara, reflects his love of the exotic and his highly individual style of painting. RIGHT: A brightly painted Japanese torii gate that once indicated the entrance to a Shinto shrine marks the Beach Entrance to the junglelike garden. Beyond the Chinese bamboo chairs and tray of seashells is the vividly trimmed and completely remodeled structure. BELOW RIGHT: Two elephants from India shaded by fringed Balinese umbrellas flank the Front Entrance. An elaborate Thai gate with cast bronze mudra hands serving as door handles opens into a tropical, walled courtyard. OPPOSITE: The open door of the Side Entrance leading from the courtyard and framing a view of the orchard suggests a living Jack Baker canvas.

OPPOSITE: *A combination of vibrantly colored elements flavors the Living Room: Mr. Baker's large painted flower panels and masses of fresh blooms, several Balinese umbrellas and the trappings of an Indian temple toy.* RIGHT: *A crab shell and driftwood with bamboo skewers holding flowers rest on an antique English pine console.* FAR RIGHT: *Beach hats, baskets, shells and signs create a casual Entrance Hall composition.* BELOW RIGHT: *Datura blossoms nestle delicately in an upturned Chinese umbrella.* BELOW FAR RIGHT: *Strands of Ethiopian beads festoon a gracefully poised antique Indian carved figure.*

ABOVE: *Jack Baker's painting of a summery garden scene blends perfectly with the lush Dining Area table arrangement of homegrown fruits and flowers, including banana tree leaves, palm fronds, calla lilies, bougainvillaea, hibiscus, avocados and lemons.* RIGHT: *Another view of the free-spirited Living Room includes the Dining Area with its antique English pine table and oak folding chairs. Adding to the exotic mélange are Chinese tortoise bamboo chairs, a Japanese lacquered tea table and an assortment of Kutch cotton-covered cushions. The Baker canvas behind the antique Chinese daybed depicts a view of Rincon Point from the artist's garden.*

BELOW: *A dressing area upstairs was transformed into an Oriental-inspired Sitting Room. An antique Chinese gilded woodcarving resembling a grape arbor and an angled mirror define the cozy niche. Indian sari fabric is used for the upholstery and draperies. A Chinese porcelain teapot filled with bougainvillaea lends brilliant beauty to a Chinese papier-mâché-incised table.*

BELOW: *While visiting, artist Charlie Brown painted the Hall with his vision of a six-foot shell found on the beach.* OPPOSITE: *On the peaked ceiling of the Master Bedroom, custom-dyed linen fabric interspaced with lacquered bamboo poles adds another personalized detail. A Venetian tôle lantern and an antique Austrian headboard fulfill the whimsical fantasy.*

**ABOVE LEFT:** *In front of the acre of property runs—or gently flows, depending on the rains and tides—a slough that melds with the Pacific waves. The beach tent can be seen in the distance.*

**ABOVE:** *Another view brings the Beach Tent, with its antique Indian handblocked canopy, into close focus. Although Mr. Baker was born in Texas and grew up in California, his love for the exotic has taken him around the world. He has lived in India and Africa. When the artist gives a party, his guests can always expect to step into an unusually striking milieu.*

As the sun goes down beyond the surf, its last rays add a golden glow to the idyllic setting for a late afternoon party. Two antique Indian toy horsemen from a Udaipur temple stand by the Beach Tent in stylish attendance, while fringed Balinese umbrellas sway in the wind and Chinese baskets laden with supplies hold the promise of a pleasurable picnic by the sea.

# ACKNOWLEDGMENTS

Many staff members and associates of *Architectural Digest* magazine were instrumental in adapting the original elements and producing the new material that appears in AMERICAN INTERIORS. We appreciate their efforts equally and thank those who were most involved alphabetically:

EVERETT T. ALCAN, Vice President Operations, Knapp Communications Corporation.

ALICE BANDY, Administrative Assistant, The Knapp Press.

SUSAN BERNARD, *Architectural Digest* Features Editor.

ROSALIE BRUNO, Vice President Circulation, Knapp Communications Corporation.

SAM BURCHELL, *Architectural Digest* Senior Editor, who rewrote and adapted the original text.

RICHARD E. BYE, The Knapp Press, Managing Director.

ANTHONY P. IACONO, *Architectural Digest* Production Director.

JOANNE JAFFE, Caption Writer.

GARRY JAMES, The Knapp Press, Associate Editor.

PHILIP KAPLAN, Vice President Graphics of *Architectural Digest* and The Knapp Press, who supervised all graphics.

BRUCE KORTEBEIN, Design Consultant.

JOHN LINCOLN, *Architectural Digest* Antiques Consultant.

JOYCE MADISON, Copy Editor.

CHRISTOPHER PHILLIPS, *Architectural Digest* Associate Editor.

HENRY RATZ, Production Director.

MARGARET REDFIELD, *Architectural Digest* Copy Editor, who edited the text.

GAYLE MOSS ROSENBERG, *Architectural Digest* Captions Editor, who supervised and edited caption material.

STUART H. SALSBURY, *Architectural Digest* Art Consultant.

JUDITH SAMUEL, Caption Writer.

ELLEN WINTERS, The Knapp Press, Assistant.

J. KELLEY YOUNGER, *Architectural Digest* Managing Editor.

# CREDITS